Well, Well, Well

I finally got best part of it all is looking up and seeing you still here with me! People who I thought... are not and people I didn't expect are here:

— Quiana, thank you for your love, inspiration, encouragement, support and wanting the best for me... I send it back to you like a boomarang that you are Blessed beyond what you can handle for you and your daughter. :)

Thank you my family and friend...

me love you

Apple

DATING MY DAD
(Trauma Bond Series)

APPLE DAILEY

Dating My Dad (Trauma Bond Series/Series One)

By: Apple Dailey

Cover created by: Anelda Attaway (Jazzy Kitty Publishing)

Designed by: Daryl Harris: www.darylharrisstudios.com

Logo designs by: Andre M. Saunders and Leroy Grayson

Editor(s): Apple Dailey and Anelda Attaway

© 2015 Apple Dailey

ISBN: 978-0-9916648-1-8

Library of Congress Control Number: 2015935997

All rights reserved. This book is protected under the copyright laws of the United States of America. This book may not be copied or reprinted for commercial gain or profit. The use of short quotations or occasional page copying for personal or group study is permitted and encouraged. Permission will be granted upon request. For Worldwide Distribution. Printed in the United States of America. Published by Jazzy Kitty Marketing & Publishing LLC dba Jazzy Kitty Publishing utilizing Microsoft Publishing Software. This book is based on a true story. The names of the characters have been changed and are used fictitiously. Any resemblance to actual persons, living or dead, events or places is entirely coincidental.

ACKNOWLEDGMENTS

I am utterly grateful to my Lord and Savior Christ Jesus and the Heavenly Father, who held me so tight during all of the storms in my life.

Thank you to Syleena Johnson for your Chapter Two album that I put on and zoned out getting this book done.

To Kem, your Kemistry and album II helped me gain an understanding of how a man should love a woman when I didn't have an example present.

To my family and friends that have supported me every step of the way, giving me space and time to get this out, thank you.

To my special Aunt Lavern, thank you for being patient and one of the biggest supporter of me.

Jaden, thank you for your youthful motivation, my nephew and little buddy.

Angela Ellis and Dr. Amanda Coleman Mason, my big sisters, thank you for your total honesty, and editing this first baby of mine.

Anelda, my new friend, sister and mentor, thank you for your inspiration; tell your hubby thanks for sharing his time with you with me.

Momma, thank you for your go-getter spirit and writing skills that I witnessed in you at a young age.

My Grandparents, I will never forget the fearless and self-less character you developed in me, I miss you both Lena and George King and I carry you both with me all the time. I know you both are proud of me.

Finally, yet importantly, the men in and out of my life, thank you for the know-hows, and the have not's, I wouldn't have a thing to write about without my experiences with you all.

I love hearing from my supporters when you get a chance, hit me up on my website at www.appledailey.com. *Also, drop me a post on* www.facebook.com/worldclassauthor *and on Instagram@Iamappledailey.*

Me love you ☺

DEDICATIONS

I dedicate this book to all the victims and survivors of domestic violence all around the world. Some of you may be gone, but not forgotten.

I want to say to you that I am so sorry the system failed you; hurting people hurt you, but it was not your fault!

Me love you all!

TABLE OF CONTENTS

Introduction	i
Episode 1	01
Episode 2 March 1986	23
Episode 3	35
Episode 4	61
Episode 5	76
Episode 6	85
Episode 7 Two Months Later	101
Episode 8	111
Episode 9	126
Episode 10	133
Episode 11	152
Episode 12	163
Episode 13 Spring of 1991	201
Episode 14 Summer of 1992	221
About the Author	248

INTRODUCTION

For Shelby, childhood was anything but guilt-free. According to her father, Spivey, she was to blame for any and everything wrong in his life. In Spivey's eyes, his daughter was never been good for anything. He tried to brainwash her with his madness. Shelby had no choice but to grow up fast. When opportunity presented itself, she took off for a chance at a life better than the one she had known; searching for unconditional love and a safe place to rest.

She thinks she has found true love, but instead she has gotten exactly what she didn't want; the kind of man she hated. Now, Shelby has to find the strength to overcome being trapped in this cycle of life!

New on the scene in the literary community, Apple Dailey depicts the consequential endangerment of a girl's relationship with her father. Apple describes in her surreal novel the trials & triumphs of Shelby, a woman's life without the true love of a father.

Episode 1

Apple Dailey

Regina knew Spivey couldn't stand the sight of me; so I don't know why she was trying to get me to tell a lie to the police officer as if I didn't see my life zooming before me. How in the hell could she expect me to forget him swinging a 2x4 board, full of sharp nails at my head? Before that, he choked me until the air in my lungs paused and he ripped off the new necklace that my Auntie Pinkie had just given me.

I wasn't trying to hit him back, but my reactions took over and I did just that, landing my fist smack dead in the middle of his right jawbone. I was trying to protect my face from the blow of the board and Spivey from possibly disfiguring me. He didn't give a damn if I was family, he was furious! He swung that 2x4 at me with all the strength he possessed. Viewers thought I was a stranger that had swallowed the last sip of his beer or worse, the last hit of his pint of Night Train, not his daughter. He was shocked that I fought him back and so was I. Humiliation had taken over, but I was too afraid to die at the hands of my inebriated father.

"Sir, he didn't mean to harm her. He disciplined her for coming in the house too late. He lost his temper when she didn't answer him, that's all." As usual, Regina jumped lying and defending her piece of man, choosing his side over mine. One officer said, "Ma'am still, it's not appropriate for you all to be outside with these shenanigans. If you want to get drunk and fight, stay in your home and not outside disturbing the peace." "What peace?" I said noticeably. Our snooping neighbors were always outside watching and talking about any and everything that crossed their feeble minds, especially Marva. She loved to sit on her decomposing porch furniture yapping and bending all truths. Regina called her the yellow pages because she knew everybody's business. There was no peace in our neighborhood, if it wasn't us, somebody else was arguing and fighting. Especially around the first of the month when the government checks came out, all we heard was laughing and partying. As soon as the music went off, the cursing and fighting began.

Anyway, I watched the squad cars pull off wishing they had him in the backseat taking him somewhere far, far away from 18th Street. Although they warned Spivey and Regina of the consequences of them coming back, I knew the madness wasn't over.

I walked slowly into the house and closed the door behind me softly, as if I was sneaking in; I was. Spivey hated it when somebody called the police on him, even if he was beating Regina blind; I had better not ever try to rescue her. Neither Regina nor I had the guts to rat him out to the cops in fear that it would be a miserable day for both of us. Spivey was the man of the house; he had to have total control over everything and everybody in it, wrong or right!

We made eye contact and I paused for a few minutes waiting to see if he was going to say something to me, but I swear my heart thumped one hundred beats per minute. I thought he would see it through my blouse and use it as an opportunity to attack me again, simply because he knew that he was able to put fear in me, but he didn't. I went on to my bedroom and plopped down on the bed to breathe a bit, before taking my clothes off. I should have taken a bath, but I put on some clean PJ's anyway. I would've had to damn near wet myself, before I'd step out of that room again.

It wasn't that I didn't love Spivey; I just couldn't find a place for me in his heart. It seemed like he despised anything and everything connected to me. He hated my dog, my cat, my friends, my mother and most of all he hated me. Once he felt I was attached to anything, he snatched it or them away from me leaving me alone to figure out life all on my own. He loved to break up the ground I walked on. He was training me for the ways of the world, as he said it. Though Regina was my Momma, he made sure that I understood she was his woman first and only my mother whenever he wasn't using her.

Through the long hard years, I developed a love-hate relationship with Spivey. I loved him for being my father and I hated him most of the time because he made it impossible for me to wrap my loving arms around him with all of the bruises he adorned me with. On top of that, he criticized whatever I did, period! I tried everything to make him love me, but he just didn't. If he did care, he had a strange way of showing it. Most of the time, I felt abandoned and alone. That's why I'd only let people in my little world just long enough to have a few laughs. Once the good times were gone, so was I emotionally; I couldn't trust anyone. I didn't think people could be happy too long without pulling you down the sad drain with them.

Though I befriended many, I didn't keep them long. If I did, just like the hand of time, Spivey would come right behind me like a clock's second hand destroying whatever friendships I built. He snatched away time I'll never get back. He'd embarrass me by jumping to conclusions or sizing me up, belittling me and assuming the worst about me. Spivey turned everybody against me, scaring them off. I tweaked the wide opened valve that pours out all of my feelings into a slow drip. I dried up any thoughts of them coming in and hurting me then taking off out of my life with pieces of me scattered all around town. I got so tired of reintroducing and re-explaining myself. I felt like a failure of a Twelve Step Program of life always trying to recover from the bad reputation that my own dad constantly put out there about me. So many people already had the evil eye on me that they were intently watching for the lies that Spivey volunteered about me, while he sipped from his brown paper bag. To this day, I still don't understand how people could believe a liar, especially lies from a person they knew to be one. Anytime someone would get comfortable with him enough and had the courage to confront him about his wrong doings, he would deny any accusations with a straight face. The entire neighborhood witnessed our family drama, at least twice a year. He was a horrible liar; he was worse than a guilty man on the witness stand heading for death row. For some odd reason Spivey thought, he was invincible and innocent until proven otherwise. My dad thought he had every right to do as he pleased, when it came to his family and nobody had a right to say anything about it.

As far back as I could remember Spivey's transformation toward me began right when I needed him the most, just about the time I became 8-years-old. I wondered if he noticed the difference in me as I had. I knew I was unusual for a child my age, but I couldn't help who I was. I was special, witty and just as harmless as a butterfly. Yet, I had the strength of an army when I spoke; the strength that he tried to break at every conceivable opportunity. Maybe that's what triggered his animosity towards me? My wisdom, strength and courtesy remained anybody's guess where it came from. I had no idea that it would piss Spivey off that much to burn my bridges with him. Though we lived in the grimy inner city of Milwaukee, I had big dreams of living somewhere else, like in one of those fancy homes on the far eastside just over the riverbanks. Regina worked a lot and Spivey had income coming in so I felt if they wanted to we could live better and not in the slums, if they chose to. Spivey hated that about me. Let him tell it, I had a chip on my shoulder that made him question whom my dad really was. Sometimes I agreed with him because they both seemed to love living in the hood and begging for what they needed and spending their money on what they wanted. Anyway, the gentleness and endurance that I held, I didn't recognize in them either. "I'm adopted?" I wished. Whom was I kidding; Spivey and Regina were selfish, poverty-stricken and so into each other for an extra addition to their disordered lives on purpose; he already said he wished I were never born. If they had another child, it would be a trial from God.

Before my Grandmother passed away, God rest her soul, she told me about my mother's liveliness before she met my dad. I couldn't picture Regina being happy, unless she was trying to keep Spivey from pounding on her. Grandma said Regina was hopping around at life like a fish in shallow waters, very unaware of the danger she was in once Spivey had zeroed in on her. "He hooked that gurl through her mouth with his popular gift of gab and carried her home draining her of the sweet innocent essence. However, once he got her alone to himself, he laid out his plans. That man spread her out on his table scraping away her identity with the sharpest blades of lies and broken promises he had. That man scaled away my baby's protective shield until there was nothing I could say or do to help her again." "He must have used some solid golden hooks Grandma?" I said as I laughed with my grandmother, but I was scared after I heard that. Now, that I think about it, she was right about Regina. Time produced days that progressed into months and months into anniversaries. For Regina, it was a very long time away from all that she had ever known and loved.

I barely knew my mother's side of the family. She stopped going to her family's functions to shelter Spivey from his in-laws' criticisms of him. Yes, my mother's family hated the day he was born. The last thing I remember my grandmother saying to Regina was, "I've done all I can do for you Gina. Your head is as thick as the skulls on your daddy's 'nem side. Thank God, your father ain't here to see the rat you let into our cozy home. He'd probably sit up in his casket, if you ever went out to Grace Moore to visit him." Of course, my mother didn't hear a word her mother said.

Anyway, I tried everything possible to stay on that man's good side and out of his way, whenever his bad side arrived, which was every day, after his first pint. I stayed busy and on the go most of the time. I was underweight from being nervous and nauseous. I walked on eggshells without crushing them so that Spivey wouldn't get pissed off at me. I attempted numerous times to make Regina aware of his offenses toward me, but as usual, she didn't want to hear it and chose to overlook all of the red flags, pink flags and purple flags too. She down played all of his foolishness, calling them mistakes. Mistakes like when he would stagger home, after a long day of drinking and after she had a long hard day of standing on her feet cleaning hotel rooms. Regina would often find pleasure in cleaning up the funky vomit he released throughout the house. She even tried to forget the deep bruises he left on her once clear and beautiful dark skin. She excused him, saying he was just old fashioned and even claimed that he was just like everybody else who made mistakes. If that's what they did in the olden days to their loved ones, I was glad to be born in the 70s. Regardless, I don't want any man to ware and tare the hell out of me with his fists, then excuse it as a mistake. Moreover, try to bandage me up with an "I'm sorry Baby." Makes me wonder, if that's the reason she took his lifestyle in stride. Could she have witnessed things such as this, when she was a child? Had she given into the lie that being committed and receiving love meant she had to endure abuse? Did Regina believe that having a man meant that she didn't exist for any purpose outside of him? Regina would bypass her gut feelings to forget his mess because she was in love with Spivey, but I wasn't and I didn't.

I remember the time in 1983, when Spivey came home with a cute big-headed puppy. He said the puppy was to be for protection until he discovered it was a fake. It was a Boston Terrier mixed with Pit Bull. He thought he had a purebred Pit; what did he expect for $20.00? I didn't care if he was a Pit Bull or a fake I loved that puppy. It was love at first sight; my face lit up, whenever I saw him. He had small furry ears and big furry paws and I loved the way he smelled. He liked to eat the hotdogs and scrambled eggs that I fed him for breakfast. I looked forward to coming home from school to feeding the puppy and taking him out to play. He was the best excuse to get out of the house and away from Spivey and his drunkenness.

I will never forget one particularly ugly day. I was a couple minutes late coming home from my first day of summer school. I had picked out some special Dandelions from the mesh for Regina and stopped at the corner store to get some hotdogs with the single dollar food stamp that I had left. I chit chatted with my meddlesome neighbors a bit then happily headed home. The house was quiet as I walked up and entered. Where was my happy puppy to greet me? I checked the bathroom, the kitchen, all over the house. I couldn't find him! I called for him several times, but no puppy. My heart felt like it was going to stop, when I noticed all of his things were gone. I knew in my heart that my pain had Spivey's name written all over it.

A few weeks had gone past my heartache from not having my happy puppy around. Now, I can admit that I felt as if that puppy loved me more than anybody I knew; at least he needed me. I couldn't stop thinking about him, wondering if he was all right and if whoever had him was aware that he liked hotdogs and scrambled eggs.

Spivey interrupted my favorite sitcom-Good Times, ordering me to make a run to Mr. Carl's corner store to buy his cigarettes. I turned the TV off, put on my Jellies and walked toward the kitchen. On my way out of the back door, I heard a soft whimpering coming from below, in the basement. Though I was scared, I continued traveling toward the sound as far as my fears would allow me. It was spooky, cold and funky, but something kept moving my feet. A tiny seam of light guided me closer to what echoed like a pitiful bark. It was a dog trapped in the small dark room in our basement. I pried open the door. "Oh my God!" I cried aloud; it was my puppy. The little fella still had a chain wrapped around his neck and when I pulled on it to lift him to his feet; the chain came loose with some of his flesh dangling in the links. I squatted down and scooped him up carrying him, feeling my way around to the wash tub to clean the blood from his wounds. The clumps of hair and rotted flesh that crumbled off covered the sink and made me nauseous.

We made it outdoors and I collapsed with him in my arms. I laid him down and ran in the house to get some towels not giving a damn about Spivey and his funky cigarettes. The puppy was motionless and damn near dead from starvation and I didn't expect that he could walk. When I got back to the bottom stair, he was standing there soaked and wet in the doorway gazing up at me with generous eyes as if he remembered me. He looked as if he had matured, but was still the same size from starvation. I wrapped him up in the towels and held him as we sat under the Apple tree.

I hid the puppy in an abandoned garage not far from where I lived. I was able to check on him every day; nursing him back to good health was a joy for me. I began re-training him and it wasn't long before he was just a cute and friendly puppy again. I decided to name him; I called him "Life." He was full of it too. I found myself confiding in him a lot. He became my best friend. We'd play together escaping the reality of the horrible things Spivey did to the both of us.

Spivey was angry, once he noticed Life sitting in the middle of the living room floor. "Hell naw! Get that mutt out of here!" Life growled at him. Spivey tried to stare him down, but Life growled again and leaped for Spivey. "No! Sit!" I commanded. Life eased down on his back paws then to his front ones laying his head down in submission to me. Not once, did he take his eyes off his enemy; from that point on, we protected each other. He had my back. Then to my surprise, Spivey went on and approved him to stay. In some small way, I believe that my dad felt guilty for trying to get rid of my precious puppy. Regardless, he was a smart animal that didn't forget. Life never bowed down to him again.

About a month later, Spivey told Regina to keep the alley cat that he found which he named "Low-Life." He lied, telling her that rats roamed our basement. Nevertheless, things were smooth between Life and the cat, whenever I was around. Low-Life slapped-boxed the puppy and bit his tail often. They chased each other throughout the house every day. It was their way of communicating, I guess. Which is why I could not accept the tale my dad told me when I came home from school searching for the cat? "Here kitty-kitty," I called as I looked all over. "I don't know whatcha looking for. That cat is dead and yo damn stupid dog ate it! So I got rid of him 'fore he eat somebody else up and you ain't got no money to pay nobody's hospital bills," he said. He told me this with a mean mug, no sympathy at all. I broke down to my knees crying. I knew if something was wrong, Spivey was the main suspect. He couldn't help himself; he was evil, filled with hate and revenge that often resulted in abusive and destructive actions. I didn't believe my dog would do such a thing; they loved playing with each other. It didn't add up right at all. I should've known he would've been up to something way before this occurred, but I just didn't want to believe my dad could be so cruel again.

Anyway, Spivey was my dad and I had to love him. I would do just about anything to keep the peace with him, even if he enjoyed hurting me. I just didn't know what to do or what would work to maintain the harmony. He was always irritated with me, even when he was sober. When he was drunk, he told me that I was a good for nothing that would never amount to anything. He said that I would be pregnant after the first sign of blood, beginning my maturity. To top it all off, he often reminded me that I was a little ugly Bitch. "You take after yo' momma 'nem side, with them big foreheads and big hands," he'd pick and joke. Let him tell it, he was just brutally honest and would rather me hear it from him because he was someone that gave a damn about me instead of a stranger who could care less. He always said that I talked too much. At times, I did. I always made some kind of effort to fill in the gaps of time between him and me. I wanted to connect with him in hopes of breaking up the cells of my growing tumor of resentment toward him.

Whenever I brought friends around, he loved to size me up comparing me to them. He'd say things like, how I should be like them and how much better they looked and acted than me. Over the phone, he'd be mean to them. "Hell naw, Shelby ain't here! And when you see her ass, tell her to come home and clean up this nasty house!" I stopped the few friends I had from calling once he hit me in the mouth with the phone. "Is Shelby there? Is Shelby there?" he asked as he repeated in a low deep tone then a high-pitched squeal, grinning, mocking the different voices of my friends who called. I laughed thinking he was teasing and ended up grabbing my mouth to catch the blood that oozed onto my chin. "I pay the bills! You are 13 with no damn job. Don't you ever forget that! And bet not nobody call here no fuckin' mo' asking for you! You got that? Now gone outside some damn where, before I draw some blood out of yo' ass!" *"What did I do,"* I asked myself in shock. He gave me a look that sent pain from my stomach into my toes. My legs took heed and led me to the back stairs and outside.

I walked to the front to sit on the porch wondering what I was going to use to soak up the rest of the blood. I was afraid that one of our prying neighbors would see me so I hopped up and proceeded to the backyard.

That's when I noticed Regina pulling up in the side driveway coming home from work. I ran to her for comfort, "Momma, look what Daddy did," I showed her as I was opening my mouth. "Back up before you get blood on his car. Let me look," she took hold of my chin while moving my head upward for a closer look. "Turn your head to the right," she examined. Regina reached in her purse, pulled out a small restaurant napkin and moistened it with a bit of her saliva. "Here, wipe your mouth, you'll be all right. You and yo' Daddy gonna drive me crazy one day. I can't even go to work without y'all acting like fools," she blurted out as she walked away leaving me standing there feeling helpless and unsure of what to do. She made me feel that I was wrong for even thinking of complaining or expressing my hurt from her man. If we were driving her crazy, we didn't have to drive her much farther for that, I thought.

I rinsed off my mouth and hands with the rusty tasting water from the outside hose then I went back to sit under the Apple tree to wipe away my tears with that same napkin that Regina had given me. I dreamt of the day when I would gain Regina's attention and persuade her to leave him and take me with her.

I surmised that Spivey must've wanted a boy and got me instead. That was all I could come up with after trying to think of options that could make things better between us: especially since, he had the privilege of naming me Shelby Spivey, after him. Thank God, it was an epicene name or he would have been calling me junior.

He also had a habit of taking me to taverns and neighborhood bars, where he would have me dance on top of the bar for silver coins and dollar bills for the regular drinkers that arrived before 5:00 p.m. They were mostly old men and low-income folks who didn't have a job or those who worked nights and hung out in the afternoons. The drinks were much cheaper back then. There was less disorder during the afternoon hours in the Milwaukee bars. The daytime partygoers loved the idea of a little girl performing grown-up dances. Spivey lied and told Regina that we were broke and in need of a hot meal after she discovered years later, that he took me to the places to wiggle what she gave me. In my young mind, I was having lots of fun going to the taverns with Spivey, especially down at the Pink Pony, where I would see Ms. Trina. She was a friendly neighborhood drunk with big breasts and everybody knew she kept all of her treasures and plenty of money hidden in them. She would give me clothes and shoes and let me go behind the bar to get all the soda I wanted, while I was there. If I didn't know any better, I would say that she had a thing for my dad. That's probably the reason he took me up there so much; I was his front. I could make some money for him and he could see her.

The Pink Pony was always full of people who loved to laugh and party while spending big money on their blue-collar budgets. It would be mostly older men with a few sharply dressed young women in the bar. I often fantasized about the day that I'd grow up and have men all over me running to do anything for me whenever I called. Ms. Trina had them wrapped around her finger. To me, she was a goddess or something close to it.

When my pre-teen years arrived, there were some good moments, every now and then. Like the time Spivey taught me how to drive because he was too drunk to get us home from an afternoon of drinking. I gave Ms. Trina a good-bye kiss and ran out to the car; sat in the front seat and waited for him. He came out searching for me through the windshield as he staggered out shouting, "Shelby! Drive! Drive Shelby!" I didn't think he was serious, but the red in his eye and the mean look on his face warned me that he was. However, he was too drunk to be anything, but harmless. He got in the driver's seat and slammed the door and said, "I'ma do the ped-o-lin' and you steer the damn wheel." I turned the key in the ignition, leaned over his legs, put the gear in D and we drove off. I was so nervous, but I didn't dare say a word about it. I didn't want him to yell at me and receive a mouth full of his boozed up breath.

This partnership wasn't going too well. "Dad!" I panicked. "I got it! I got it!" he responded waking up out of his drunken slumber. After two more attempts at navigating the car down the street, I threw the gear into P and I snatched his drunken ass from the driver's seat. The next thing I knew, I was actively manipulating the gas and brake pedals driving us home by myself. Even with his big gut nudging me in the back, after he fell over on me, while I was driving, I was still able to reach the pedals just fine. I'm not tall now and I wasn't tall then. I prayed to God that no one would notice that I was a thirteen-year-old driver taking my drunken dad home.

Although those seemed like good times then, so-called good times never lasted too long. Regina laughed loudly, almost choking off her cigarette smoke as Spivey told her the story the next day of how he drank a fifth of gin, but managed to drive us home. He said, "I moved my hand like this, just like the Masons said to do if I ever got pulled over and I swear the police let us go! Didn't they Shelby?" He lied some more, waiting for me to join in. I couldn't continue with the lie, even after

Apple Dailey

Regina gave that signal for me to go along with the flow. I didn't say a word because I wanted recognition for driving us home, but as usual, he needed all the glory. "See there. I hate this little Bitch! She always gotta fuck shit up for me, with her fast ass!" With that, Regina tried to rescue the situation. "Spivey she didn't hear you, finish telling me?" "Naw, go get my damn belt so I can put a smile on this little Bitch's face!" Regina vaulted to the room in compliance. As long as it wasn't she this time around, she went gladly on her way to get his leather belt with the big buckle on it.

"You bet not cry, either," he warned me. I was tired, sick and tired of getting bruised up because I wouldn't do wrong or overlook and forget his mess. In the back of my mind, I counted the stairs I had to hurdle to get out of the house. I had to make sure I could clear them once I ran. "Spivey, where did you put it?" Regina stalled and that was my queue. He was a fool to think that I was going to stick around again for a punishment I didn't deserve. He took a few steps toward their bedroom and I took off like a frightened mouse in the opposite direction. I didn't know I could unhook that chain and turn that doorknob as fast as I did. I leapt the stairs four at a time falling through the screen door as if I was in an action movie getting thrown out of a bar. Off I went. Where I was running? I didn't know and I didn't care, as long as it was as far away as possible from that man.

I had been at my Grandma's house with my Uncle Les, since the day I left. Uncle Les had inherited my Grandma's property. Almost immediately, I had to face another situation. School was starting in a few days and it didn't take long for me to realize that I was virtually on my own. I didn't have any new clothes or shoes to wear. I had cut my old high water jeans to shorts and I had been washing and wearing the same two white tee shirts.

Thank goodness, work and my dad occupied Regina's days, she didn't have time to care that I was doing my own hair. My cousin Jill could have braided it, but she moved way across town. It didn't really matter, because I managed to keep up with the girls my own age, when it came to hairstyles; one ponytail to the back, side or top, worked for me as long as I could afford some of the customary Murray's Grease that black folks used to slick their hair down, at that time.

For some reason, I had lost some my hair on the side of my head. I hustled up some extra money unloading carts for older people at the grocery stores, and with the money, I bought a grown-up box perm and put that in my hair. Then, Uncle Les told me about Grandma's hair remedy, Sulfur 8 grease. I used it to help grow my hair back, but it smelled awful. There was nothing youthful about it at all. Nevertheless, I was overjoyed that my hair had grown back. Now, being responsible for my own clothing was out of my league. My parents had every excuse in the world for not purchasing new clothes for me. Even Goodwill was too expensive for them. Spivey never had a steady job. He'd work a job for 90 days all the while thinking of a way to get fired so that he could receive unemployment benefits for the next year and a half. To me, he never stopped working, judging by the way that he supervised Regina and me around the house. He always had something for us to do. Even after Regina had worked all day long, he'd manage to find something extra for her to do and like a fool, she did it. She would wash his funky feet, braid his nappy beard and clean up his hangover liquids. That would never be me, I dreaded!

Since I had left my parents' home, I was able to manage, even though they were non-supportive. My Uncle Les borrowed some money from one of his girlfriends and he bought me a few new outfits, four pairs of shoes including gym shoes and a pair of GQ kicks with the dry ice heels. "This ought to hold you over until yo' momma 'nem come and get you," he said as he handed me the shopping bag. I was happy to receive anything and from Uncle Les, I was more excited because he wasn't responsible for doing anything for me. He was on a fixed income and a penny pincher, for sure. His income was so low that, if Grandma would've left a mortgage, he could not have afforded to live there. Each year, he scraped and hustled up for the property tax.

Even though it was hard on him for me to be there, he enjoyed my company anyway. I had been the only grandchild to visit, since Grandma had passed away. We found company in each other as we went grocery shopping or watched the news and old western movies together. I also enjoyed doing things around the house. I liked helping him out in the yard, picking tomatoes and frying the green ones in egg and cornmeal batter for a snack. Truthfully, we enjoyed each other's companionship. It was peaceful and quiet, especially since his only child Jill, moved in with her new boyfriend. There wasn't any loud talking and tale telling, no drunken men hanging around slapping five all day or the customary saying, "excuse me" 20 times a minute, trying to get his words out right. No fighting or cursing either, I was at ease and didn't want to go back home.

Then came that dreadful day, I could have used the bathroom on myself when I saw Spivey standing in the doorway looking like Goldie the pimp with his hat all tilted to one side. He looked just as mean as the day I left, with that fake grin on his face. "Thank you for keeping Shelby while we got things together." "No problem at all," Uncle Les calmly said back. "Oh yeah, here's the new address to our home too," he handed a ripped piece of paper to Uncle Les with an address that I didn't know, which was supposed to be my new home. "What you mean new home?" Uncle Les jumped in before me. "We moved yesterday into our new house off of 29th Street. It's big, too. Big ole' Bae windows, it's nice. You should stop by and have a few cans with me one day when you not too busy?" Spivey explained. I could've fainted. I asked my Momma to move a long time ago to the far Westside of town into a nice two bedroom that she could afford easily by herself, if she had to. But, I knew he was going to talk her into moving into the inner city just so he could be close to his drinking buddies. I hated him! He was selfish and only thinking of ways to benefit himself, coward! It's all Regina's fault for spoiling him as if he deserved it. Hell, he didn't have any steady or good income to be in charge. I didn't either, but I wanted the best for all of us.

Uncle Les was a sweet old man and he didn't want any trouble. He just wanted the best for his sister and his niece. He let me go with Spivey and didn't ask for anything or put up a fight for me. "Me love you Uncle Les and I will come and see you as soon as I can. Okay?" I gave him a big hug, picked up my little plastic shopping bag full of stuff and left out behind Spivey.

The ride home was quiet, at first. Then Spivey turned the music down low telling me what he wasn't having out of me in the new house. I think that he did it just to see if he could get a reaction out of me. He talked as if the house was a diamond in a rough neighborhood and I would be some type of Tasmanian devil that would tear it down. When we pulled up, the appearance shattered all my hopes and the interior was no better than the outside. A curtain and not a door secured my room. My bedroom wasn't a room; instead, it was a spacious hallway to the front door; next to it, was the dining room where I was sure he and his drunken associates would use to hangout. My parents had the convenience of having a bedroom next to the bathroom, but I would have to walk across everybody to get to it. The carpet looked as if it must've come from the late 60s. It was a shag blanket with an explosion of colors, mostly red and orange and another color I could not make out. The wallpaper was sickening as it was an orange and purple mess! I didn't believe Regina could have been in her right mind to agree to come to a place like this. We would have been better off packed in Grandma's garage.

According to Regina, it wasn't any of my business, but she explained to me that the old property owner sold our old house and only gave 7 days to find something else.

I found out from my old neighbors that they had seen a Granger Moving Company truck in front of my old home. Granger was a company that had a contract with the county and if you ever saw that truck in front of your house, it was clear to the entire community that you were evicted. Nevertheless, none of that really mattered to me. I didn't care about what they did with the money that she made and the little he had coming in, I didn't care about her lying. What made me angry was that as my parents, they would choose such a roach-infested spot that they would call our new home and then brag about it to my Uncle Les as if we were moving-on up. There wasn't anything new about that house, except us being some new fools to move in it!

"Momma, where's my dresser and headboard?" I asked distinctly Spivey was just waiting for me to say anything so that he could snap at me. "What the hell you mean! Where's your shit! Was yo' ass over here and helping us move?!" My body stopped moving giving my brain time to catch up to the path he was trying to take me. "No, sir. I didn't know y'all was moving," I answered. I wasn't asking for trouble, but it found me anyway. "This the best we can do right now and if you don't like it you don't have to be here, dammit!" Spivey stood up staring me down like the western TV shows he always watched. I turned my head and stepped back a few steps into my room to hide my anger.

I stayed in my bedroom for hours setting up stuff and decorating the best I could. My stomach bubbled from holding my waste for so long. I wanted to go to the bathroom, but Spivey hung out in the living room and had invited some men over that he didn't even know. They all had a brown paper bag, twisted at the top that they drank from. Cigarette smoke dangled in the air and seeped through the curtain into my room. I sprayed some freshener a few times, but it didn't help. They smoked and I sprayed; they kept puffing away and I kept spraying.

At some point, I went to take a peek from the front door to survey the neighborhood. Looking left to right at the noisy neighborhood, I gathered that the people in this neighborhood must have been on welfare or they worked low wage jobs. I had no proof, but there was something about the way that they looked and the way that they dressed that led me to this conclusion. I saw two young women leaving a house from across the street wearing Milwaukee Brats and Burgers uniforms. Some kids were out in the middle of the streets, riding their bikes. One boy was riding a ten speed with dirt bike parts mixed in it. That's a bike with a big wheel in the back and a tiny wheel in the front. A couple of houses down, in an empty field, kids were wrestling, hitting backward flips on a dirty old mattress and laughing. I didn't want to go out there or meet any of them. Although it wasn't much, I missed our old house and neighbors. I wanted to leave now, but I was stuck.

Episode 2

March 1986

I didn't realize that I had kicked that ball so far across the playground. Nobody wanted to go after it so I went after my own ball. Kazeem handed the ball to me with a smile. I couldn't even hold my head up or make eye contact with him. He was good looking! Back then, I really didn't know what sexy was, but if it had anything to do with him, he was it. Kazeem was a member of the Dream Sickles drill team performers. They did everything but expose their private parts at their shows. The group was ten handsome young men that every girl in town dreamed of being with one of them, hell all of them, any one of them. Kazeem was somewhat different though, he stood out from the others. He was taller than the rest of them, jet-black smooth skin with a pretty smile to match. He looked a lot older than his team, with his full dark beard trimmed like the entertainer and sex symbol, Prince. Actually, he was a taller, dark-skinned resemblance of the Pop Star; everything about him said that he was a die-hard Prince fanatic. Kazeem was the bold one of the group that brought excitement doing things to make the girls scream for him. While watching him perform, you could tell he was more sexually experienced than the rest by the way that he moved. However, you couldn't tell if he was an adult or not. The only thing they had on Kazeem was youth. If you didn't know him you'd have thought that he was competing for the spotlight that he already possessed. In actuality, the Dream Sickles came across as seven teenaged young men and three little boys. A rumor began to spread that Kazeem was an adult, but the promoters lied about his age to keep him in the competitions. They all appeared grown the way they handled themselves, twirling around and about like exotic dancers wiggling what their parents gave them. Truth be told, I didn't think the little boys were pure virgins.

Anyway, I was daring, so I touched him on purpose. I could've melted. Instead, I grabbed the ball and turned away blushing. None of the neighborhood boys ever took any interest in me. I had developed the dreaded "ugly complex" from the things Spivey had said to me on a daily basis. All I had going for me was a rather well-developed butt that I inherited from my mother's side of the family. My rough teenage acne didn't help, either. I usually beat up the boys that I knew as they always tried to tear me down by calling me names such as, "Sand paper face." They would do anything to insult me because I was so competitive and I enjoyed beating them at any games we played. I didn't care as long as I won the game.

Why Kazeem took a liking to me was puzzling to me and it blew my young mind, and just that quick I began imagining him as my boyfriend. I wondered what it would be like to be his girlfriend. When I turned to walk away, I had hoped that he didn't notice me in my silly daze.

Had I just felt a soft brush against my butt? I attached that to my daydream. I kept walking, pretending not to have felt a thing, which was a big fat lie. That was the first time a male had ever touched me in such a way and I liked it. I felt a wet spot in my panties as I sat down on the bench while I waited for my turn to kick the ball, again. "What's wrong with you- you all to yourself? You bet not make us lose this damn game, I know that," Addison picked. There was nothing I could say. I believed that I had a crush. Hell, I was in love, at the very first feel from a male and it was nobody's business but mine. I snapped out of it briefly and responded: "Nothing. I miss living over here, you know?" I switched, throwing her off. I really did miss hanging with Addison because she was my best friend, my sister. I wouldn't have traded our friendship for anything in the world. Besides, her family took me in whenever Spivey would put me out after a stomach full of liquor. I wanted to live with Addison and her family permanently. I had known her ever since she and her family relocated to Milwaukee from Chicago around seven years, previously. Addison was the youngest of her three siblings and the only girl. Her brothers treated me like I was their little sister too. We had a lot in common. We were both tomboys, but of the few young girls in the neighborhood, Addison was the most developed. Like me, she wore baggy clothing and gym shoes, but you could still see her body frame. Addison was shaped like a grown woman, like her momma, she was what they called "big boned." One ponytail, white long tee shirts, baggy jeans, and a fresh pair of Converse were our dress code. No dresses, no stockings, no skirts and no tight pants, everything had to be loose, nothing uncomfortable. We wanted to play and play hard is what we did. Letting boys hump and grind on us wasn't our forte. Well, not then, which is why I had decided not to tell her what Kazeem had done? Addison and I reminisced a bit about our good old days living so close to each other, how we use to walk over each other's house in our pajamas. Too bad my family moved thirty blocks away.

 Suddenly, a burnt orange color took over the sky that alerted me that it was time for me to head home. Kazeem saw me getting ready to leave and made his way over to me to say good-bye. I thought I was going to pass out from panic. He put me in the hot seat by saying bye to me. He even threw in a perfect-ten smile. The moment he was out of our view, Addison started drilling me for answers that I just didn't have. "What the hell was that? When did you start seeing him? Ain't he too damn old? How old is he? Why didn't you tell me you and him were going together?" My head was spinning. I was just as caught off guard as she was. "Walk me to the bus stop Addie?" I needed some air and we were already outside. I was glowing. I was the happiest I had ever been. I shared a bit of my happiness with Addison as we waited for my bus to come. Although she was concerned about his age, Addison was content because I was happy. She made me reinstate our vow to staying a virgin until we turned eighteen. "Gurl-all them tramps gone be mad at you, when they see you with Kazeem," she agreed slapping five with me then hugging me good-bye. I smiled back at Addison and got on the bus.

"Either she goes or me, Regina! I pay the damn rent around here and ain't no child of mine gonna be talking back to me! Hell naw! Hell naw! Heell no! As a matter of fact, you got ten minutes to get yo shit and get the fuck out little Bitch!" What kind of man was he to put his only child, his daughter, out in the streets in the dark? What kind of man was he to demand my momma to choose between her offspring and his stupid guidelines? I searched for love and understanding in my dad's eyes and found none. He wouldn't make eye contact with me until he ordered me out. I couldn't cry even after I looked to Regina for help. If only she could've stood up for me once, I'd feel some kind of love. Honestly, I had a place of relief in my heart. I was tired of trying and my feet suffered from the pins and needles I walked on for his love. At 15-years-old, I wanted better. Maybe now I could live with Addison's family and be happy.

I held the few things I possessed tightly as I bent down to kiss Regina.

"I'll be at Addison's Momma, if you need me," I informed her, hoping to ease her mind of worrying about me. "Two minutes left Shelby," Spivey coached. I didn't take the time to say goodbye to him. I stared at the back stairs for a moment. Accepting that this may be the last time I saw them. Down those stairs and out the door was a mystery. I really didn't know if I could leave home. "Ouch," I let out after hopping the flight of stairs. My home hadn't been a comfort zone, it was insanity. Moreover, leaving it meant being free of it; beginning something new; something uncertain; but I felt I was up for the challenge.

I roamed the streets for hours like a loosed dog that had been chained up for years. As time fondled me closer to midnight, I became more alert and afraid. By this time, I had walked my way out of my new neighborhood and was way across town with no bus fare and exhausted. My Aunt Blu, Spivey's sister lived nearby, but she had just given birth overnight. It was too late to show up at her house unannounced. I needed to get to Addison's house and catch her mother to ask her permission face-to-face, if I could live with them. I had to show her the pain in my eyes and feed her answers to the questions she's always believed about my dysfunctional family, that her daughter wouldn't give her. I stood at the bus stop hoping to stumble on someone at his or her final destination. I could ask for their transfer and they'd slip it to me quick enough. I had it all figured out. I'd pretend that I was running for the bus, I'd get on, show my pass and be on my way.

I should be in the bed right now with the fan blowing over my hot body, not planted in this grassy field drunk. I didn't have the slightest memory of how I got there, where I was or what happened. The taste of dirt sickened me as I exhaled, blowing mud out of my mouth. The aroma of liquor left me hanging and wondering what I had to drink. My thoughts were blurred. My head felt like it was racing around a track going nowhere but in circles. I used what bit of strength I had to pull myself up in a sitting position. I blacked out again.

His voice sounded familiar, but he kept moving. I closed one eye to focus. "Kazeem? What happened?" I asked. Confused and mad, ready to fight assuming he was the reason I was in this field. I couldn't win a fight with a stuffed animal in the state I was in, but I was going to try. I changed my mind because I was at his mercy. Whatever he had done to me, I couldn't feel it. I was okay and alive. I didn't feel bruised up and from the looks of things all my clothes were still on and in place. Kazeem fell to the ground in laughter. "You don't remember?" he asked as he kept giggling. "Remember what?" I smirked too. "Little One, you almost got hit by the bus and was so shook up that I took you to the liquor store, copped some beer to calm you down. I can tell you weren't use to drinking Little One the way you guzzled that 40 ounce down." Why is he calling me Little One? Don't matter; it sounds welcoming and attaching like we blended even though we're from two different walks of life. I thought maybe he would be conceited or snobby, not at all. Kazeem was warm and generous of himself. He wasn't untouchable. In fact, I swore that he had a liking for me as thick as my crush for him. I must've been too excited as I babbled at the mouth. He knew so much about me. "Where are we?" "Around the corner from your house; look, there's Carl's Store," he said as he pointed assuring me, again that I was okay. "I know it's late, but I don't want you to go home like this. From what I've heard your father is an asshole. If he ever puts his hands on you again, I'ma kill 'em," my eyes bucked. His statement was sobering. How did he know? Why did he care so much to say such a defensive statement? "I don't live over here anymore. My Dad moved us about a month ago over to near Center and April Ave. Dad don't mean no harm, he's just old-fashioned," I said. I thought how I reminded myself of how stupid Regina sounded after defending Spivey. I had hoped that I didn't come across to him like Regina had to me. "Where were you on your way to?" he asked me with a concerned look on his handsome face.

Upon that question, I laid back onto the grassy field. At that point, I really didn't care. I was safe with Kazeem from any crazy night stalkers, rapists and murders. I just needed to let the liquor wear off. "Nope get up. Let's take a stroll. You need to walk it out of your system," Kazeem said as he lifted me up by my arm, held me tight and began walking me. "I'm going to Addison's house down the street from here?" I instructed him. "Be careful. Don't bump your head," Kazeem said as he directed me into his room in the basement through the weak window. I was concerned for myself, maybe a bit scary too. He was weird to me. I've never seen a fanatic like him. His basement didn't look anything like mine. Magazine clippings, drawings and pictures of Prince, Vanity 6 and kinky naked women collaged on his walls. Strawberry incense hung heavy in the air. It smelled good though. I almost kicked the space heater over while taking inventory of my surroundings. He really adored Prince and Jimmy Hendricks. He dressed like them, sounded like them, performed like them. At that point, I understood why Kazeem was so seductive and tranquilizing.

"Here, eat this," he said as he startled me out of my nosiness, poking me softly in my side. He held a plate of chopped up fried hotdogs and instant whipped potatoes in my face. "I can't eat. I feel sick." I lied, I wanted to haul that food down my throat like it was the last meal on earth, but not in front of him. "That's the reason you need to eat something," he insisted. "I have to use the bathroom," I asked. I needed to see how I was looking and practice eating in the mirror. "My parents are here and they're a trip so you have to keep it down and use it down here. Over there in the sink," he pointed. "I can't use the bathroom in the sink," I doubted. "Oh, you got to do number two," he said as he sympathized, smiling at the same time. "No, I just don't want to do that." What an awkward situation. However, the more I turned to look over there at the sink the more I had to go. "Okay, where are you going, while I use it?" I couldn't dare go to the bathroom in front of him. "You could mess up your insides holding it like that, trust me I know. It's tissue over there to wipe yourself." "Kazeem? Where's my change?" a female voice broke up our conversation. He put his finger near his lips signaling for me to keep quiet. "I'll be right back," he whispered. I stood there frozen stiff concentrating, so I wouldn't release urine from my body. The pressure was intense. I couldn't hold it any longer so I leaped over near the washtub, opening my pants dropping them and my panties to my knees. I gripped the tub tightly to keep from falling backwards as my clothes and feet hung. You could hear the relief in my belly with every ounce I let out.

I heard him coming down the stairs, but I was too far into my release to cut it short. Kazeem walked over near me. I thought he was going to push me or play around. He reached behind me to turn the water on. I was fully embarrassed. Either he's done this before, or it really didn't bother him. I jumped down searching around the area for the tissue trying my best not to make eye contact with him. I'd probably burst out laughing, something I've always done instead of blushing. I caught the roll he tossed to me. "Don't put your clothes back on," he said softly. What in the hell was he up to? I'm not going to stand up here naked. If Addison got a hold of this scene she'd run it every day, all day like re-runs of her favorite TV show. "What?" I asked. "Ain't nobody gonna do nothing to you. I brought a hand cloth and bath towel so you can wash up. Remember, you were spread out all in the grass and mud. I thought you might want to clean yourself up." Yeah, I thought, but cautioned why he was so thoughtful and kind. Maybe he was as innocent as me. He appeared so mature because he was concerned. Compassion is one of the required steps to maturity.

What could I say to that? No, I don't want to clean myself up? He slid his way over to me so close that I was inhaling the aftermath of his fried hotdog breath. He stood tall above me. My eyelashes tickled his chest. I wanted to run, but where. Daylight seemed so far away and so desired. Kazeem lathered up the rag. I reached for it. I wanted him to move away from me and go up the stairs; anywhere. Instead, "take off your T-Shirt," he said in a deeper tone. Tears slid down my face. I discerned domination in his request. "Why are you crying? You act like I'ma hurt you or something. I just wanna clean you up Little One," at that moment, I despised that name. He gripped my jaws lifting my head up, "How old are you Shelby? You're acting like a 5-year-old." "14." I lied, I was 15-years-old. Regardless, I was too young for whatever he had up his sleeve. "You're only three years younger than me. I'm not going to hurt you at all,

I promise. Look at me." This time he used one of his fingers to lift my head. I backed up against the cold steel washtub surrendering to him to wash me up.

Kazeem performed when he wasn't on stage. He bathed me in the fashion of a ritual. He undressed me and got on his knees. My young body experienced warmth never known. He touched my special place passionately as he cleansed it. I was afraid to tell him to stop and yet, I had never felt so cared for. I couldn't recall the last time I had a hug from a male, let alone a soft touch. His mattress sucked me into a fetal position ready to sleep like a baby. It had the scent of baby powder. The pillows puffed out sweet smelling herbal hair grease. Kazeem's silhouette transpired a man, not a boy. The height, broad shoulders, thick calves and his private part was long and chunky with a curve in it. I must admit it was the first time I ever wanted to go home. Part of me was comfortable, but the fear of the unknown ate away at rest. Kazeem did everything to put me at ease. I felt I would be okay as long as I did what he asked because I was on his turf. I was with a mannish boy about to spend the night. Spivey would beat me until the blood came from my pores, if he knew this. "Thank you Kazeem," I honored. "Thank you for all that you've done for me. I wouldn't have thought you to be this down to earth. As soon as daylight hits, I'll be on my way," I negotiated as he fed me my plate of food he warmed up for me to finish. I fell fast to sleep in his arms after eating with his naked body against mine.

One night turned into three days. Not once did he ever try to get sex from me. We played board games, watched comedy shows on his fancy VCR, raked leaves for his parents and neighbors and he gave the profits to me. He gave me horseback rides to and from the store. Surprisingly, Kazeem understood me. I finally relaxed and put my guards down with him, submitted and accepted his help. Clearly, he didn't want anything from me, but my company, plus to protect me from anything possible. His heart manifested his gentleness and how underappreciated he was. I felt that his differences were misunderstood. One day, I decided, I was going to show him that it was my privilege to know him and suck up the air he exhaled. I desired to be free just like him. He received me. We bonded in those short moments as friends. He cared for me and I treasured him. Bonnie and Clyde would be an overstatement, what we had was simply and sensually Kazeem and Shelby. Kazeem had sneaked to use his parent's washer and dryer to clean my clothes. The entire time I was there, I wore his big shirts, shorts and socks. I didn't realize that I'd been gone that length of time. It seemed too soon. It was time that I showed up somewhere near home. I couldn't stay in his peaceful palace forever. He packed a book bag with juices and sandwiches for our journey. I had money but he wanted us to walk to my side of town. He too, enjoyed my stay; his mission was to savor every second with his newfound friend. I was a bit worried that someone would see us together, pushing us to the front center of their conversations. Kazeem dressed like a Punk Rocker and me, a tomboy. We didn't get too far, before the cackles began. However, he controlled the chatter with the raise of one eyebrow. I wondered, if he had done that on purpose to show me his power with that "you Tarzan, me Jane" mentality. Though he was gentle to me, he had the ability to throw people off with a mean look just like my dad; I think that he sent chills down their backs as well.

Episode 3

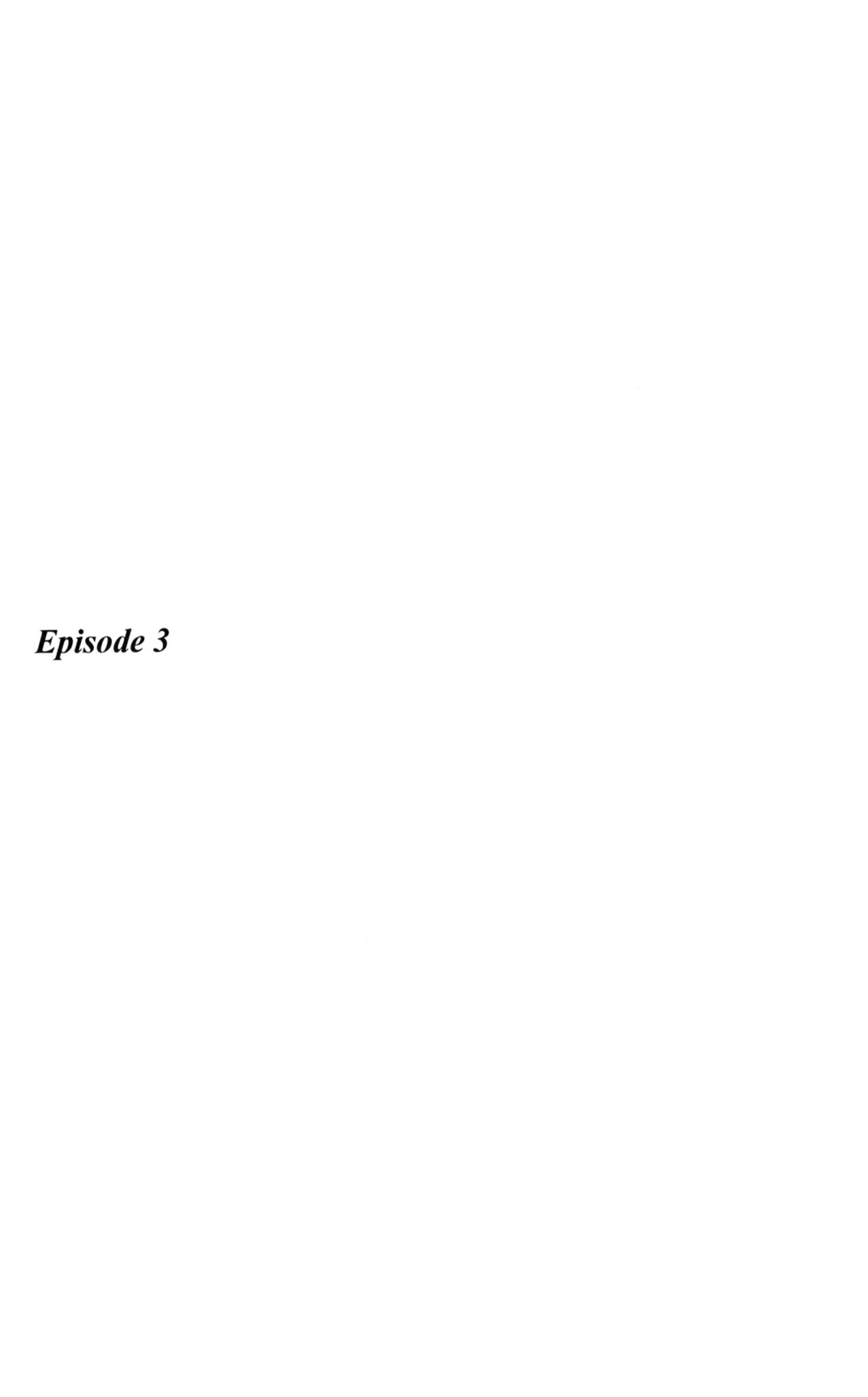

Dating My Dad

I hated living with Agnes and her mom, it was always chaotic. Strange men knocked at the door at all hours of the night. The constant interchange of visitors made it very difficult for me to get a good nights' sleep for school. Rest escaped me because I was too occupied listening to the loud, passionate, symphonic noises in the middle of the night. In addition, the few clothes that I did have were slowly disappearing. Living with Agnes and her mom gave me a pure picture of the false image that Agnes presented. I saw Agnes' life in 3D and it wasn't pretty. Spivey always compared me to her, he'd put me down but, he'd build her up. He'd yap about how pretty she was and how she was gonna grow up and have whatever she wanted in life because she was going places.

Agnes loved to repeat the good things my dad said about her in front of the neighborhood boys. She used his words to try to tear me down only to thicken her shallow ego. Spivey was a master at manipulation. He set a trap designed to reveal Agnes' very own insecurities and weaknesses and she fell right into it. She also attempted to pull me in with her; that's how I saw it. But, I was wiser than my years and I learned to numb myself releasing all of the power her words may have had over me.

Anyway, living with the two of them did a lot to lift my self-esteem. I realized that just because a person appeared to be in a better position than me, that's all it was…just an appearance. I had sympathy for Agnes and I understood why she was so quick to put others down. She was afraid that people would see her flaws; her line of defense was to get to them first. I'm glad that I spent some time with them and got to see things with my own eyes, had I not, she would've received the worse beat down she'd ever had from me and Addison. I wondered if Agnes was afraid that I'd blurt out all of their ugly family business above the loudness of our mutual gathering spots. I didn't have to; she was good at exposing and making a fool of herself without any help from me.

The coldness and unwanted welcome from her mother always sent chills through me, which kept me alert and on my toes. Whenever I mentioned to her mother the possibility of my leaving, she would insist that I stay. She would tell me that it wasn't a problem with me living there. I think she just wanted me around so that she could keep an eye on me for my dad or keep him coming around. If I didn't know any better, I'd say she was screwing around with Spivey too. They drank together, they joked together, and they went fishing together, often.

I wish I could've stayed at Addison's house, but they had fallen onto hard times with a house full of people. Her uncle and his family had beaten me to the vacancy at Addison's place. I even thought about staying at my grandmother's house with Uncle Les, again, but that would mean that I wouldn't be able to see Kazeem on a regular. Uncle Les was old school and traditional, he wouldn't dare have some grown looking boy visit his niece. I decided that I'd stick it out with Agnes 'nem because anything was better than going back home with Spivey and Regina again.

I saw Regina driving down North Avenue. She must have been going home from work. I phoned her to let her know that I was all right, but the thought of her not giving a damn caused me to drop the receiver. I didn't bother leaving a message. I reassured myself that her days were full with Spivey's demands.

My dad pretended not to see me, but his cold recognition stabbed me in the back like a steel-tipped dart, as it interrupted my conversation and caused me to turn around abruptly. In my eyes, I was all grown up now and didn't owe him anything. It's not like I did anything to him you know, he put me out. He cursed me, too. He was the destroyer of what little family we did have. It would have to be a cold day in hell before I bowed down to him again. Yet, I had so many questions. What did he expect me to do? Surely, not walk into another one of his blackouts of beatings! Besides, he could have shown me that he cared a little about me. I was his 15-year-old daughter; for once, couldn't he have been the one to initiate reconciliation? Why couldn't he have been the one to admit his wrong doings? Why couldn't he have been my loving dad instead of hating me? Guess not. The prideful strut he took past me said it all. He didn't give a damn about me. I blurted out, "I'm fine too! I love you and miss you too! How are you Spivey?" I made sure he was far enough away to give me a head start if I needed to run. I heard a familiar voice. "What was that all about? Did that mutherfucka do something to you?" Kazeem asked, as he approached me. "Naw, I was just angry with him and he couldn't care less," I sobbed. "You'll be alright; don't worry. He'll come around. A man's got his pride but, your dad is a real asshole," he said. Kazeem's assurance felt good as he pinched my butt and gave me that grin of his. I had grown to like him a lot and I was comfortable with him, but I have to admit that his mannish behavior still bothered me. I enjoyed talking to him and I liked that he listened and gave decent advice. I just didn't want him touching me all the time. Whatever he had in mind for me, I wasn't ready for his grown ass to penetrate my young body yet.

    My weekly routine at Agnes' consisted of getting up at 6:30 am, showering and dressing...no breakfast, chatting with Agnes' mom for a few minutes while she sipped her black coffee and fussed at the morning news for exposing the entire ghetto in the worst ways. I heard the squeaking of the weak wood on the porch that signified Kazeem was there to pick me up for school. "See you later," and out the door I went. Kazeem always had a sugary donut and a small carton of 2% milk in hand for my breakfast. We'd talk and giggle on the way to school. He had dropped out of school as a senior but he made sure that I was going to finish. In unspoken words, he had become a father figure, but at the same time, a boyfriend to me. He let all the boys around me know that I was his and that I was not to be touched. The boys still said hi but that was about it, except for one. During the first week of school, Rodney Chapman asked me for a pen and I began to look for one in my book bag. While I was searching for it, Rodney took it upon himself to grab my butt. It infuriated me and I walked away, giving him a pass, but that wasn't the end of it. Kazeem had a look out named Chico and Chico went and told Kazeem what had happened to me. Kazeem confronted Rodney and while Rodney tried to give his explanation, Kazeem hit him in the mouth and beat him up badly. I got suspended for a few days because it appeared to the principal that I had someone come up to the school and fight for me. If only they knew, I had let it go.

Nonetheless, each day after school, there would be Kazeem waiting and grinning with a McDonald's Happy Meal bag and soft drink in his hands. We'd ride the bus down Fond du lac Avenue to the Eastside. Kazeem had a disabled uncle named, Kaklin who lived on the eighth floor of one of the East-side high-rise apartments down there. The complex was for the elderly and disabled, not for the drug-infested fanatics that crowded

Dating My Dad

the area. Needles, broken cigarette lighters and chewed up gum greeted you as you entered the smelly elevators. Uncle Kaklin told me that he'd been using heroin since the 80s, after he got shot in the elbow. "Those damn medications that they give you don't work on your pain. Hell, all they wanna do is get you hooked on them prescriptions to pay their bills." I felt sorry for Uncle Kaklin, but his pain was there before I knew him, there wasn't anything I could do about his problem except pray for his best. Kazeem told me that he was helping Uncle Kaklin by checking on him and making sure that he ate, but after a few visits, I soon realized how Kazeem supported himself. He was manufacturing and selling Marijuana from his uncle's apartment and he would give Uncle Kaklin a couple of leftover plants from the crop he grew for allowing him the access.

There was a spare room in his apartment and Kazeem had use of it whenever he was there. You could tell that Kazeem had ownership of the room by the bizarre posters that covered the walls. During the week, however, it was my study room. I'd be in there for hours doing homework and reading steamy novels. About 8:00 p.m., Kazeem would pop in to hand me a plate of food that he had delivered, good stuff too. My parents never ordered out and we never went out to dinner, but Kazeem fed me nothing but the best every night, before taking me home. He'd have a big wad of money that he'd peel away a ten-dollar bill to pay the Johnnie Cab driver; these were the customary bootleg or uncertified cab drivers that everyone used. "I'll see you in the morning Little One," he'd say, then kiss my forehead and waited for me to get safely into the house, before jumping back into the Johnny Cab driving off.

My leftover meals were precious tasty morsels to Agnes. "Damn, he got it like that? What do he do?" she'd ask as she gobbled down every bit, leaving none for her mother. "Pul—ease," I responded. It was none of her business. "What do you mean? He has a job," she said. If she knew about the money Kazeem really had, as hungry as she was, food wouldn't be the only leftovers she'd want. I didn't have to worry, she wasn't Kazeem's type. According to him, she was worn out, used up, tainted and good for nothing, but to skeet on. This was why he was looking for me a new place to stay because he didn't want me around her. Until he succeeded, he made sure I only slept there. He approved of Addison since she was still a virgin and she didn't draw much attention to herself because she was a tomboy.

He didn't mind me hanging out with Addison for a few hours each day, but the rest of the time was Kazeem, Kazeem and more Kazeem. Most of the time that I spent with Addison was when he was down in Illinois with his connections. All I knew was that as soon as his brother's Cadillac Deville crossed the inner city lines of Milwaukee, Kazeem wanted his Little One at his side. Whatever we were going to do after he arrived back in town, he had it all planned. It appeared to Addison that Kazeem was madly in love with me, and she thought of me as a man-freak.

I loved the fun we had; the new stuff he introduced me to, like going to Six Flags or the summer carnivals and walks along the Michigan Lake Pier. Kazeem even took me to the Humane Society to touch the exotic animals. He had a finesse about him that caused older people to respect him, although I had heard rumors of him being a bully. Even though he was large and angry looking he seemed as harmless as a kitten to me. If he had the ability to hurt someone, I didn't see it. All I've ever witnessed was the softer side of him, at least until Agnes had gotten jealous and pissed him off!

One night, Kazeem allowed me to go to one of JC's basement parties. Everybody from the neighborhood was there. The DJ was playing all the old jams and some new stuff that we had never heard. Most of the boys had forty-ounce bottles of Malt Liquor on hand and some passed them between each other. The girls were shake-dancing and popping every muscle they had, competing against each other for the boys' attention. You would've thought we were in some sort of a raunchy strip club. One girl took off her shoes to get down, hitting the splits and another girl stripped down to her bra, panties and socks. This caused the crowd to hover around them while provoking them to take off everything. Addison and I got pushed to the back of the crowd and we couldn't see what was going on. The next thing I knew, Agnes came rushing towards me yelling, "Run Shelby!" Addison grabbed me by the shirt and snatched me to the corner for cover. People were screaming and smashing into each other as they were trying to get out the door. I learned later that some well-known troublemakers, Nickel Bag and his crew, had tried to bust their way into the party without paying. There was resistance; they tussled with the woman of the house. Some of the rowdy group managed to get inside, but others were busted before they could get into the party. Those on the outside were furious that they couldn't get into the party so they kicked in some windows. Somebody lit some paper and rags on fire and threw them into the basement. There was smoke and confusion everywhere. As soon as we saw our chance to get out of the unruly place, Addison and I made a mad-dash towards the door to escape. We made it and we were relieved that we had gotten out of the building. As Addison was brushing off her clothes and I was trying hard to the catch my breath, I heard, "Shelby! Come over here, now!" I faintly recognized that familiar voice calling me. My eyes pierced the surrounding houses to see who it could have been. "Over here!" Then, my eyes settled on him. It was Kazeem and I could tell he was worried, but the look in his eyes also said something different…he was angry. "What happened?" he demanded. I tried to explain in detail what had just happened, but he wasn't really listening. He had this odd look on his face, as if he didn't believe me and I wasn't telling him the truth. "You got all your stuff?" he asked. I nodded, yes and said, "Let's go." We took off walking and I didn't get a chance to say goodbye to Addison. At that moment, though he had scared me so bad that I didn't have time to concern myself with how Addison was going to get home because I was worried about me and what was in store for me.

"Where are we going?" I asked as I noticed that we were passing Agnes's house. Oh, well it was the weekend, I didn't have to go to school, but I wanted to go to Agnes's to get away from Mr. Unpredictable Kazeem. "Just come on!" I followed him to the liquor store and waited outside. I stood against the building with my head down. The last thing I needed was for someone to recognize me and then Kazeem catch me communicating. When he returned, he had two 40-ounces of Malt Liquor. He cracked them both open as we set off to an undisclosed destination. "Drink!" he said. He shoved the bottle into my chest as if it was my own. "I don't want it. I don't want to drink beer. I don't want to drink anything." "What did I say Little One? Drink, before I fuck you up!" he yelled. He was serious and I felt that I needed to comply. "Why are you acting so strange?" I asked him just before taking a sip of the beer. Although he had cursed at me, his profanity towards me didn't seem as harsh as Spivey's, I rationalized. "Drink some more!" he said as he frowned and raised his eyebrow. I took a big swig. It was bitter. The foam made me gag and some of it bubbled out of my mouth. He stood over me until I drank half of it. I began to feel light headed and cold. "Kazeem, I think I'm drunk. Can you please take me home?" I begged. It seemed he didn't have an ounce of sympathy toward me, but rather a ton of anger. Kazeem had transformed into someone who I no longer recognized. I had never seen him act that way before. He wanted me sloppy drunk, but why.

I had an instant flashback of that night that I was drunk in the field. My conscious thoughts told me that he had gotten me intoxicated on purpose that night. At that precise moment, I blurted out, "You think you slick? You're the one who got me plastered so that you could take advantage of me, you liar, you!" I stared at him face-to-face with my hands on my hips leaning hard to the right. In another instant, I stood there in disbelief of my thoughts that those words had escaped my lips. Then I felt the sting…Whap! Shining blue spots covered my eyes. I took off running in circles. Everything was blurry. I didn't get far, I was abruptly stopped by Kazeem's arm around my stomach. "Sit down, you ain't going nowhere!" he yelled as he pushed me down. I looked up as tears ran down my cheeks. I wanted to get away from him so that I could forget the whole thing and just rest. Instead, visions of my mother's torments from Spivey invaded my conscience. The more I looked at him the more he resembled my dad…big, irritated, unpredictable and scary!

Kazeem groped me all over while he stimulated himself. His touch made my flesh crawl, as if a caterpillar was exploring my body. I didn't move. Through my eyes and tears, I begged him to stop, all the while hoping that he'd understand what a big mistake he was making. I wasn't ready for the purposes he had in mind for me. "Open your shirt," I didn't move. I kept weeping. He grabbed me by the collar and yanked me to my feet. "Stop!" I snapped, but this man pulled and dragged me all the way to his house. He shoved me through his basement window. I hit the floor like a clump of mud. After he jumped in, he left me sitting in the middle of the floor while he went up the stairs to check to see if anyone was at home. Hah! I wish I could have seen the look on Kazeem's face when he returned to find me gone. Somehow, I gathered strength from my fear. I hoisted myself up, pressed my bare feet against the wall and got the hell out of that dungeon. I ran as if I had just committed a crime and the police were right behind me, but I didn't get far. I was still tipsy and very tired from the beer. Some wonderful person a few alleys down, left their overhead garage door up. I ran in and pulled it down while I stood there quietly in the corner listening for footsteps.

"What the hell!" the woman of the house shouted, finding me sleep stretched out on top of her car with blue tarp covering me. "Oh Ma'am, I don't mean to scare you. I hid in here because I was running from some man who was trying to rape me." "I'm sorry, Praise the Lord!! Honey, where's your shoes? Are you all right?" her voice shifted from frightened to friendly. I said, "I don't know all I did was run. I'm sorry, your door was open and it saved my life." "Do you know who he was?" she asked. My face said yes, but my mouth told her differently, "No Ma'am. I didn't see him because I was running so fast." "Edwa-a-ard! Mr. Edward," she called her husband. "He came out into the garage. He seemed to be relieved to hear that something had happened to me instead of him being in some sort of trouble.

"Come on in the house young lady, we'll call the cops and you can stay with us until they come," he said as he put his hand around me walking me towards their back door. "Thank you, sir, but if you don't mind, please don't call the police. I don't want that man to know where I am. It wasn't far from here where he was chasing me," I was spooked. I assumed Kazeem would be on the lookout for me. Besides, whenever Regina or the neighbors would call the police for help, the police would come, but it was only to irritate and agitate Spivey even more. "Baby you should call the cops, but if you don't want us to call them, we won't force you to," the nice man replied. I asked if I could use their phone to call Regina. "You sure can Baby," he said. His wife handed me the phone and then began to fix me something to eat and drink. While I was waiting for Regina to answer the phone, I looked at what appeared to be photographs of their family reunions on the kitchen walls. They had a large family and everyone looked as if they were united and happy.

Regina didn't answer. I rationalized that she must have still been at work. "Do you have the time Ma'am?" I asked as I opened the napkin wrapped sandwich that she had put in front of me. I took a big bite as she sprang from her highchair to find out the time. She and her husband were so kind to me that for a second, I wished that they were my parents. I could fit right in, from the looks of things; their children were all grown and gone. "One thirty in the afternoon," she graciously replied. "What time does your mother get home from work?" the husband asked. "About four o'clock, sir. By the time I get there she'll be home to open the door." "Well, you make yourself at home while you're here, we'll get you home safe and sound," he concluded.

I still had butterflies from the scare last night; Kazeem showed me that he could be a monster at any given moment. During the entire incident, he never told me what the problem was, he just snapped! I reorganized that maybe it was the Malt Liquor. After all, Spivey use to see rats in his dreams whenever he ate pork and drank Malt Liquor. Still, I wasn't going to be no Regina and let a man beat on me. I'd kill him or myself, if it came down to it.

Time evaporated. I felt so safe and special at the Edward's home. Mr. Edward cleaned some fish that he had caught and his wife showed me how to cut and gut them for freezing. She was thoughtful and sharing. She shared with me how many children and grandchildren they had. She told me they had been living in their home for forty-six years and counting. Her husband had built their home with his own hands, but when he retired they used some of his pension to get their home professionally remodeled. She showed me her garden that was full of vegetables and flowers, she reminded me of my Grandma. With heartfelt sincerity, I said, "Ma'am, too bad I wasn't born in your family." "Awe Sugar, that's so sweet of you to say, but it's not who you come from that matters. The most important part is that you're here and where the Lord is going to take you," she smiled. *"Her words stuck to me like grits and cheese. She was right, but, how was I going to get myself out of the current situation,"* I thought.

Never had I had a ride so smooth and comfortable. Mrs. Edward's

Lincoln glided like a boat on easy waters down the mean and bumpy streets of Milwaukee's inner city. It skipped the mean ugly potholes and hugged the corners. I waved proudly at a few known classmates and neighbors as we cruised by. Agnes' mom licked her lips and fixed her wig, when she saw the big white Lincoln pull up in front of her house. She frowned when she noticed it was a female driving, as I stepped out of the passenger side. I asked Mrs. Edward if she wanted to come inside for a moment, but she declined. I didn't blame her for not wanting to park her car and come inside their disorderly house. The chances would've been slim that her beautiful Lincoln would've still been where she parked it when she came back out.

"Where you been Miss Thing?" Agnes's mom asked, while she sucked her teeth as I passed by her saying hello. I continued, "Long story Ma'am," as I headed towards my bedroom. "You know I'm responsible for you? I know you think you're an adult, but you ain't. That grown looking ass boy-man has been over here a million times looking for you. He looks like he lost his puppy. You just missed him. He said he'd be back and I got $20.00 from him, we ain't got no food. You hear me Miss Thing?" My heart pumped faster. Everything she said was distorted until she mentioned getting money from him. Of all of the men, she has slept with, why would she have to get money from Kazeem, my man? On second thought, who cared? I didn't. "I'm going back home to my parents," I said. I informed Agnes of my plans as I packed up what was left of my things. "Oh, your Dad said you could come back?" she picked. I told her that I hadn't spoken to Dad, but that I had to go back. I asked her to please not tell Kazeem where I had gone if he came back looking for me. I didn't tell Agnes the reasons for my returning home because it was my business and not hers. I didn't trust her with that kind of information anyway. She was the neighborhood gossiper and she'd enjoy spreading my business around like the sheets on her bed. She was sloppy and messy, to say the least!

Agnes passed me without speaking or saying a word as I dragged my plastic bags of belongings to the car. "Momma, where's she going?" Agnes yelled back toward the house. "Chile…I don't give a damn," her mother returned to her. It was then that I noticed that she was out of control with anger. Suddenly, Agnes leaped up the stairs and charged at me. I sensed that she was angry with me for leaving as I walked out the door and down the walk toward Mrs. Edward's car. As I got to the car, I saw Mrs. Edward raise forward. I knew that she was witnessing the exchange of words between Agnes and me. "You bet not take those curlers!" Agnes yelled at me. I told her she could have them and that they were on the bathroom counter. "I bought them, but I never used them, remember? Enjoy and good bye," I said as I put the rest of my stuff in the trunk of Mrs. Edward's car and closed it. I walked around to the passenger side of the car and slid in. Then we drove off. It was then that Mrs. Edward said, "Praise the Lord, Shelby. Then there are people who hate you. I'm glad God got you away from there," she confirmed.

Spivey and a few of his drinking buddies were sitting on the front porch when Mrs. Edward and I pulled up. Each one of them cuffed their brown paper bags of liquor tightly while they lowered them from Mrs. Edward's sight. Spivey's eyes bucked a bit as he was unaware of the identity of this stranger who was bringing me home. I hoped they'd recognize her as the church going woman that she was and show a little respect. Humph! What was I thinking? Spivey didn't respect himself let alone some woman he didn't know? He wouldn't care if she had been Mother Theresa standing next to God, if she was a female, then she was beneath him. Luckily, I had already primed Mrs. Edward for the performance. She had a hunch what it would be like, she said. But she hadn't seen the likes of Spivey in living color. "Hey Shelby," George King said grinning. He was always nice to Regina and me. If George King was around when Spivey got drunk and started picking on me, he'd tell my dad a thing or two about himself. Of course, Spivey would state his claim and demand that George King leave. I was just happy that somebody stood up to him. "Hi Mr. George King," I waved. Spivey stood up and leaned over the banister. He spat out a big glob of saliva through the gap between his two missing front teeth like a snake shooting out venom that landed about ten feet away. I hated it when he did that. It was the most disgusting sight, especially when he did it in front of a woman.

"What you want?" Spivey asked me as he ran his dirty hand across his nose wiggling it and loosing up some more mucus to release. "Hey Daddy, is Momma home, yet?" I said trying to overlook his insult and repulsive behavior while attempting to calm the awkward moment. "Do you see her?" he answered sarcastically. If I could have turned to run at that very moment, I would have. Somehow, my gut told me Spivey was glad to see me. I smiled. Mrs. Edward let down her window and called me back to her car. "Look here Sweetie, I've got to get back to the house because Mr. Edward needs to take his insulin shot. But here, I wrote down all my information and ways for you to contact us if you ever need something.

And don't worry about your dad he's just bitter, but it's not with you. Look at him for God's sakes, he's destroying himself with all of his drinking and carrying on. You keep your head to the sky because I'll be praying for you. And remember, the Lord don't like ugly," she said. Fear gripped me as she helped me to unload my things and place them on the curb. My heart wished I was going back home with her.

I stood still next to my bags searching in a two-block radius for any distractions that would get the stares from Spivey and his crew off me. He was so unpredictable. There was no telling what he would try next. My arms stayed relaxed, afraid of being rejected if I made the first move of grabbing my belongings to carry them into the house. "You need any help Shelby?" George King asked, sympathizing, breaking the icy standoff between Spivey and me. "No thank you Mr. George King. I got it." "I don't know where she thinks she's going with them bags. Sho ain't in here, since she been gone, my wife and I been good...real good!" he responded to George King as if I hadn't been standing there listening. I knew Spivey didn't care, I just didn't understand why I still did.

Things simmered down a bit after Regina came home. I was still sitting on the curb watching the cars roll by and waving at acquainted people in the neighborhood when Regina walked up behind me and stood over me to kiss my forehead. "Hey curly top," she said to me as she acknowledged the change in my appearance. She hadn't seen me in a couple of weeks. I had filled out somewhat from good eating that Kazeem supplied to me and my hair grew out because of the Jerry Curl. I was proud of my curl. I sat three hours to get it done. I was also hoping that she would have noticed the fear and stress in my face once I looked into her eyes; she didn't. Why did I expect that she would rescue me while she was tucked away in her own bondage of denial and dread? Maybe if I told her what had been going on with me on a woman-to-woman level of communication, she would understand and she would allow herself to break free and save her only child from following in her footsteps? Nevertheless, of course, that level of communication and understanding would be ignored, as usual.

"You'll be alright, that's how all men are. You'll get use to it, it won't hurt long, men get better the older they get. That's why you got to stay home under your daddy so he can protect you," my mother said. I couldn't believe my own mother was coaching me into getting my ass kicked for the rest of my life. Not once did I ever see her smile from any of the blows Spivey delivered to her body and face. Moreover, not one time had she ever thanked him for any of the abuse either! What I had witnessed was cruelty from a human being to another, from a man to his wife, with a trunk full of fear and pain. How dare she invite me to endure such a dreadful lifestyle! In addition, the added insult to that conversation was that I had never felt protected by Spivey in the first place. Rather than feeling protected by Spivey, Regina and I were both in a desperate need for constant protection from him! If you ask me, we needed two restraining orders and 24-hours of surveillance cameras for our peace of mind and personal welfare.

As usual, Regina broke her promise to me by telling Spivey exactly what Kazeem tried to do to me and I wasn't surprised that Spivey was not pleased at all. Regina and I were his personal punching bags and nobody else's. Spivey rounded up his crew and they jibber jabbered about what they were going to do if they caught up with Kazeem. It was as if Spivey was the commander of the assignment and his personal flunkies followed. "Don't nobody put they hands on my seed but me," he announced. I could hear him pounding on his chest like a big brown gorilla. "When I see that tall ugly McDonald pimp, I'ma crack him upside his head for being with my 15-year-old daughter anyway!" he yelled as he went on to demonstrate how he would take on his opponent by punching at the air as if he was the star in a Rocky movie. I thought to myself, *"Why doesn't my dad talk to me?"* The way he was carrying on you would have thought that we were so close that he would have wanted to at least talk to me and hear what I had to say. My dad thought that he had the low-down on Kazeem while he described him in full without ever looking over at me for confirmation.

Anyway, Spivey and his bunch hung out front on the porch until dawn rehearsing repeatedly their imaginary plots of finding Kazeem. They rehearsed them so much that I was finishing Spivey's sentences to myself. They just kept on and on with the senseless rhetoric, but not one complaint was ever made to the police. And to top it off, they had the nerve to start singing…singing as if they were a group of harmonizing singers. Their behavior was disgusting.

Regina and I had a somewhat restful night. We chatted for a little while, but during the entire conversation, my eyes stayed fixed on her, I thought…*she has changed*. I could tell the stress of dealing with Spivey alone had taken a toll on her. Thank God, her buttery brown complexion remained the same, but, her eyes were framed in dark circles. She looked like a golden pancake with a frowning face scribbled on with thick dark maple syrup, her skin sagged and eyes were sunken in.

Dating My Dad

Regina had hope or she was living in a fantasy world because many of the compliments she often gave to Spivey where done with a fake smile or smirk as if she didn't believe a word that she was saying, neither did I. It was strange because she really had these hopes of him transforming into the man that she often spoke about to me, so did I.

We were in the new house, but not much had changed. Once again, the police made the trip to our home for nothing. I tried to help my mother out by demonstrating how the phone cord had been yanked out of the socket as I was making the call to them. As a witness and a victim, I was never believed and the sun was always the only other witness left to verify and expose Regina's old and fresh bruises. Thank God, the State of Wisconsin had finally changed the law concerning how officers respond to domestic disturbances. After the laws changed, it meant that disconnected calls to officers like the ones I'd made would require that they call back and if no one answered, then the dispatcher had to send out a squad car immediately. I wished that that system had been in effect previously because it could've saved Regina from being thrown into the floor model TV, headfirst. I was grateful for their rapid response this time, even though she didn't press charges. They came just in time before Spivey started up on me. I gave them details hoping they'd take him to jail for the night or forever. I enjoyed seeing Spivey submit to the harsh tone that came from one of the male officers. They called him a coward. "Woman beater," they'd taunt. One of the tall Black cops dared Spivey to hit him like he hit Regina and me. Of course, Spivey would deny putting his hands on either of us. "Man, they're lying through their teeth," Spivey plead. Overall, I felt better just having them there.

Man, I hated when she protected the monster that just finished beating the hell out of her. "Well, he didn't see me. He thought I was a stranger coming in the house so he grabbed me." I wanted to smack her for covering up for him. I didn't give a damn if he was my dad or not, to me he was a nasty creature…named Spivey. Did he show any concern for her when he popped the skin open right above her eyes? No, he didn't. If my man ever put his hands on me, I'ma kill him, I told myself.

I took the pink sheet of paper from Regina that the officer gave her. It had a court date on it. If I had to dress up and make an appearance as her, I would. She's going to be at court and she was going to press charges before Spivey killed her. They gave a green piece of paper, which was a list of battered women's shelters. She liked to wave it in Spivey's face to let him know that she had some place else to go if he acted up again. Truth be told, she wasn't going anywhere. Regina didn't have the power to leave Spivey and if she had, he knew where all of the shelters were anyway.

She tried to escape a few times to the women's shelters that were close by our old house before, but he memorized all the addresses. He used his gut feelings to sniff out her fears leading him to the very spot she was hiding. The rest was history; she could've gotten a cavity from all of the sweet-talking that he poured out to get her home. I believe Regina would go to the shelters sometimes just to get some attention from Spivey. She wanted him to love her, to recognize her and respect her, but he didn't.

Over the years, I think that his drinking deflated his brain cells because he'd forgotten how beautiful he thought she was when he first met her. He had forgotten about what he had to go through to woo her from her people's home to his. He failed to remember the promises he made to her if she trusted in him. Once the honeymoon was over, so were his promises. The liquor became his lover, the love of his life, his alibi and his courage. It seemed that after Spivey hit thirty-five his life changed. He was a big disappointment to himself and to us as he lost the tavern that he had worked so hard to get. He was a man of determination as he started out vacuuming the floors and eventually, gained ownership. However, as time and people's interests changed, so did Spivey's customers. His high profile friends evaporated like the wads of money that he use to have.

I remember how Regina was there for Spivey. She built up her man. She went from being V.I.P to R.I.P because in the process, she gave up on herself years ago. She tried to keep him on his feet, but she couldn't compete with the sparkling swigs that turned into giant gulps that Spivey had used to minimize his own fears and demons. The only thing that he could think was to beat his failures into Regina's head. He hated that she still saw him on top of his game when he knew that he had hit rock bottom. He didn't want to hear another pick me-up line of encouragement from her. He couldn't give her what he didn't retain inside…strength and courage. It just didn't exist.

"Ma'am, are you sure you're going to be okay? We can take him to jail right now for the night giving you time to think things over, if you'd like?" an officer said as he held Spivey by the collar like a school-child caught skipping class. Of course, she assured them, she was okay, but I wasn't. When they left, I went out the door with them. I needed to get a cigarette. I didn't quite know how to inhale yet, but I felt relaxed just having one or two puffs every now and then, especially when I sensed that my relationship with Kazeem could head into the same negative direction where Regina and Spivey stood.

"Your dad smokes Winston's. Who are you getting these Newport's for Shelby?" the gas station clerk asked. I couldn't think of anything to tell him so I yawned and mumbled; "my uncle is visiting." I hated that Spivey knew everybody no matter where we moved to. Anyway, I opened that pack of cigarettes as if they were pieces of candy that I had been craving for weeks. I lit one up right in front of the store. The smell of the menthol relaxed me as soon as it hit my nose. I held the smoke in my mouth until I got across the street blowing it out as if I had been doing it for years. I decided to stroll around the block so that I could inhale at least two more cigarettes before going home.

The summer air brought peace to my skin; I held my arms up and opened like the wings of an airplane letting the breeze take control of my muscles. It was my favorite time of day; sunset, just before the night closed out the beautiful day. The sun was a burnt orange color; it had followed me as I walked. The sound of car horns from the cuties blew at me on Center Avenue. I put my head down and kept walking and my butt switched harder the faster I walked. Center Avenue was known for prostitutes hanging out and picking up tricks so I wanted to get off that street as quickly as possible, plus I needed to get home to check on Regina.

It was quiet in the house. I stood on the garbage can to look inside. Regina was lying on the couch watching Maude. Spivey was searching the icebox for a cold beer. *"Hmmm, at least they're not fighting,"* I thought. I hopped down from the tin can. As I bent over to lift the can up to take it to the back alongside of the garage, I felt somebody grab my neck as I turned towards the house. I couldn't scream because a hand covered my mouth. I struggled to release the grip to escape. *Tears ran down my face as I thought of being raped and literally murdered outside of my own home.* "Don't move!" he groaned at me. I kicked and I bit his hand. I gripped the concrete to gain my balance, but he snatched me back with his strong hands. Oh my God, it was Kazeem! I cried even more discovering who the predator was. "When I move my hand, if you say anything, I'ma punch all your teeth out of your mouth," he warned me. I nodded in agreement. He lifted me to my feet by the throat shoving me into the garage. "Where you been Shelby?" Kazeem didn't look like himself. He looked like some kind of sniper. His mouth was dry; his lips were white and peeling as if he had been picking at them. His hair was all out of place, it looked like he hadn't put a comb through it in days. He smelled like old beer. He had the nerve to say that my breath stank. "What the hell are you doing smoking cigarettes?" he demanded of me. I was so nervous my words shivered and went back down my throat. His grip got tighter around my neck stalling my words from their path, surrendering them out of my mouth. "I've been here," I exhaled. He let go, took a step back, looked me over and forced me onto an old car. Kazeem warned me that I was his and his only as he stripped me of my clothing. He forced himself inside me pushing out my innocence, turning my beautiful dream of woman-hood into a dreaded nightmare. I felt like a doe that had been preyed on and caught by her hunter. A fish swimming freely then snatched up in a net. I was unaware of the ending, but it didn't matter because I knew I'd never be the same again.

    He surged in and out of me for a little while, but it felt like hours, then

Kazeem let out an "Awuuuh." He removed himself from me pulling me closer. He jerked a little and relaxed the rest of his funky fluids on top of me. He felt like dead weight. We were sliding off the car. He caught me, stood me up and looked me in the eye. "Whenever I come to your window, you come outside or I'm a kill your daddy. Oh yeah, and tell that mutherfucka if he wants some of me, come up to the courts around the way...old ass," as he snatched up his pants and showed me his gun. I stood there blank. "Put your stuff on, I'ma watch you until you get in the house, Little One. I miss you. Don't try that shit no more, okay?" I wanted to slap him. Instead, I put my things back on disregarding the wet stuff that covered my private area. My walk was slow, but steady. I could feel the painful form of his big penis as if it was still inside me.

I sat in the tub of water for an hour. I lathered up and scrubbed myself like a doctor preparing for surgery, only to smell his scent still stuck to me. Not only was Kazeem controlling my thoughts he had taken my body captive and was seeping out of my pores. I ran even hotter bath water and plopped in it hoping to scorch my skin and erase any traces of him from the inside and outside of me.

I said nothing to my parents. They were busy making up. I could hear Regina forgiving Spivey in every passionate stroke he gave her. I went on to bed frightened and confused. I stayed up all night twisting and turning, I kept bumping into my invisible wall of what did I do. I couldn't break through. That transparent wall allowed me to see that it was safe for me to believe that I didn't want what had just happened to me, nor did I ask for it. Nonetheless, I kept bouncing back and forth between its boundaries. I must have done something to cause this. He wasn't the Kazeem I knew.

What did I do? Were there limits that I should have remembered? Yet, I didn't have the answers. I chased the answers, but they ran and hid from me and kept me up all night searching for them. I was like a zombie living in fear the next day. Even Regina and Spivey's arguing and breaking household goods couldn't penetrate my fears. I completely ignored them while lying in my bed in silence, with the curtain opened as I stared at the ceiling.

Episode 4

Nothing got pass Addison. She was like a machine sorting mail by the barcode and the 9 o'clock news. However, I considered Addison a real good friend, which is why it didn't surprise me that she was the first person to notice the change in me. "Uuuuh. You been having sex, ain't cha?" she picked. I smiled, yet searched her eyes, hoping I could trust her with the truth. I had been masking my forceful fears and I programmed my pains to hurt when I was alone. If only she knew, I wanted to tell her, but I was afraid for her life, as well as mine, if I did. After all, Kazeem had made it clear that I was to tell no one. I wish he had told me how I was supposed to hide the spread of my hips, the sway of my strut or the aim of my new conversation. I wasn't naive anymore and I couldn't conceal it.

Spivey assumed and blurted out in an intense argument that I was doing something. He thinks that his threats toward me stopped Kazeem from operating and performing surgery to my body, changing me into his special work of art, his new creation. I was a mess inside. At that point, I understood why Regina hadn't been herself in years; once a man has a plan for your life and none for his own, nothing will stop him. Kazeem definitely had one for me.

I decided that to share my disarray with Addison would not be best for all concerned. I loved her and all, but, I was too embarrassed and too uncomfortable with it myself to tell her the real deal. I preferred that Addison remains in the same role of my journey, as usual. Besides, she was the only connection I had left plugged into what my life should have been like at our age.

I turned to face the new direction signaling that I was changing the subject and she followed my lead. We went on to our hangout, the courts, sat on the benches and watched the boys play. She wanted to roll a few balls down the concrete lanes, but I wasn't feeling up to it. I sat there rehearsing how just a few months ago, I was as innocent as the frightening screams we yelled at the cinema while watching horror flicks. I wondered if Kazeem had his eye on me the entire time. "Shelby?" Addison called, snapping me out of thought. "Whats up?" I gave. "Girl, there goes your friend boy," she giggled. I turned to see who she was referring to as my friend boy. Kazeem, I ducked down in the benches hoping to hide from him. He hadn't seen me until big mouth pointed me out. "Kazeem? Here she goes!" Addison yelled across the playground to him like she had known him all her life. Although, I had never mentioned him having sex with me, she knew that I had a crush on him at one time and now to her, we were boyfriend and girlfriend, but that wasn't it at all. I knew by the expression on his face that I was going to have to explain her actions or pay dreadfully for them. Amazingly, he kept on walking over to the basketball courts. A sigh of relief seeped from my heart out of my mouth. Addison asked, "What's wrong with you? You act like you don't want to say nothing to him. And he walked away like he didn't know who the hell you were." I played it off like I was uncomfortable. "Girl pul-ease don't do that. I don't want him to be with me, up here. You know Daddy will kill me," I bluffed. "Oh, 'cause I was about to say something crazy to him," she replied. I couldn't help but to love Addison. I knew that she loved me and that she never meant any harm. Addison was a good friend of mine and I wouldn't have traded our friendship for anything, even if I had to keep a secret to protect her and me.

 Addison and I headed back towards her home, as we noticed the sun's yoke split and spread into the sky. We decided to hang out at the corner for a bit to watch the cars drive pass, while she grounded me with the latest news of the neighborhood. I was on full in less than an hour of listening to her. "Shelby?" a familiar voice called, interrupting my feast of whispering bubbly. Addison smiled, rising up from the concrete standing at attention. "What!" I snapped. "I'ma let you two talk, and I'll see you tomorrow Shelby," Addison bailed out. She confirmed my thought of who the voice belonged to. "Don't leave, stay here please?" I mumbled to her. Addison caught the hint that I didn't want to be alone with him and I was so glad she stayed.

I twisted my body around to face him. My stomach was weak and I was lost for words. "Hey Kazeem, whats up?" I asked smiling as he came closer. It was a sure sign that he was aware that he was annoying me. I wished him away, but he wouldn't leave. He was like a painful sticker bug. Anyway, he kissed me on the forehead and asked what we were doing hanging on the corner as if he didn't know. He broke the chill of my cold emotions that only he sensed. Before I could answer him, Addison went to him like he was her best friend. I let her go.

We all hung out and laughed on the corner awhile. I speculated Kazeem putting her at ease by painting a fake portrait of us, presenting a much better image than my being a victim of his madness. Let him tell it, he was the best thing that ever happened to me. Superman couldn't provide protection from Spivey that Kazeem proclaimed to have been. Of course Addison fell for it. Her mind was still young and she was blinded by his Dream Sickles performances. I knew differently because I had been living in a nightmare for the past few weeks. Kazeem was a fraud and a predator. The crush I had was overcrowded by the drama and the pain that was hidden behind his false presentation.

Silence fell between us after Addison departed. I tried leaving with her, but he grabbed my hand and pinched it hard signifying to me to stay put. I watched her all the way to her front door, wishing I were with her. "Why have you been so quiet?" he asked with a smirk on his face that I could have slapped across the street and stepped on it then squashed it. "No reason," I replied. "Let's go to my uncle's house?" "You know that I can't go. My daddy is probably looking out for me as we speak," I said. I was staring at his raised eyebrow and before I could focus on his eyes, he was in my face with his hand lifted. "Hey muthafucka! I told you to stay away from my damn daughter!" Spivey roared, catching Kazeem and me off guard. I've never been so happy to see Spivey. He was my hero, had it not been for his sixth sense and his presence with that iron bat in his hand, ain't no telling what would have happened to me.

Spivey raised his bat higher and charged full speed ahead at him. Kazeem punched me in the chest, grabbed me by the breast and dragged me along with him. I screamed and struggled, falling as he pulled me. I wasn't going! Thankfully, I slipped out of his grip. He glanced back as he took off running. "Don't you let me catch yo' grown ass around her no more!" Spivey's voice echoed as it trembled my soul. "Get up. You aah right?" he started on me. Spivey was in rare form. His chest was poked out and he was breathing hard. This was the first time I've seen Spivey stand up to a man for any female. Conversely, on the way home, he talked to me like it was my entire fault. "Yo' ass is grounded. I told yo' Momma that you hot in the ass. I knew something was going on. I knew it," he kept repeating. He didn't even bother asking me my side. But it was okay, 'cause I was safe and on my way home.

"Shelby, you're going to stay with your Auntie Pinkie for a while. She'll keep an eye on you and you'll be going to a new school and all, once you get settled in," Regina told me. I detected Spivey was the root of this decision. He was a coward and still bitter with me from the last time I called the police on him. He was in need of any excuse to send me away. I rolled my eyes at Regina. She didn't respond, knowing she was wrong for agreeing to send me off. She protected that man at all cost. She didn't care, if he was a hopeless scary drunk. He was her poor excuse for a husband that needed her and she wasn't letting anything come between that. Not even me, their only child.

I packed so fast you would have thought that flood waters were gushing through our house. I was mad and ready to go. I was too mad to re-call my adventure with Kazeem. And I had been through too many let-downs with Spivey and Regina to think that they were looking out for my best interest. In light of it, I was excited about getting away and starting fresh. I was glad that there would be no more Kazeem around to hurt me. My Auntie Pinkie lived on the other side of town where very few Blacks lived, so I knew I wouldn't see him there. He stood out like a dreadful weed in a fine-looking flowerbed.

Auntie Pinkie's appearance had changed. She looked a lot slimmer and younger since the last time I had seen her, which had been about four years ago. She still wore hooker red nail polish. She changed her hair from red to strawberry-blonde, it lightened up her skin a few shades. Auntie could easily pass for 20 something. She had some new spunk in her and seemed glad to have me over. Auntie Pinkie had no children; it was just her and her two tiny wiener dogs, Sassy and Kingston. She had a long time boyfriend (Jelly) who came to visit her on the weekends, pay her bills and such. I wondered why they never got married. I liked Jelly; he was respectful, thoughtful and kind. He treated Auntie Pinkie like a baby doll. For the most part, he was calm but very opinionated after drinking his expensive wine. He told a lot of sex jokes too, while under the influence. I didn't care, as long as they were laughing and enjoying each other and his words weren't directed at me. Compared to my parents, being over there was heaven.

I'm not sure if it was in Auntie Pinkie's plans to befriend me, but she really seemed to care about me. She broke down the lines of limitations and asked me about what I knew about the birds and bees. Auntie Pinkie was patient and she allowed me to respond and talk in my own pace. I opened up and let her have exactly what she wanted from me…the truth. The more I opened up, the more I got to know her. I bounced to the point of actually wishing that she was my mother. "Auntie Pinkie, did you ever want kids?" When I fearfully asked this question, I was uncertain, if she thought that I was being disrespectful or if she thought that I was being nosey. "Yes, I did, but I had an accident, when I was little. Therefore, I wasn't able to have children." *That wasn't enough; I had to know the details. What a shame,* " I thought to myself. "Why are you looking at me like that?" she asked as she got up from the kitchen table to go over to her pure white doubled door refrigerator. I just sat there with a blank look on my face. Man, was the pressure on to ask her one more question. I inhaled deeply, my breath stopped when she began to question me. "Do you drink?" she asked. The look on her face told me that she wasn't speaking of water, juice or pop. She was asking me about heavy recreational beverages. I didn't answer, I just smiled. I held my tongue, but I did want something strong to drink to knock down that wall of fear, for sure. I just didn't know how to answer Auntie Pinkie. Then she said, "You have sex and smoke cigarettes so I know you done had something to drink. You're 15, not too far from 18-years-old, one more with your Auntie Pinkie ain't gone kill you…and neither will I." I stopped holding my breath and answered her question, "Yes, I'd like a glass of whatever you're having, please." She handed me her bottle of JB Scotch and a short glass of ice. "Pour to your satisfaction," she offered. I didn't know whether to have a little or fill it up. I glanced over at her glass to measure for a respectable amount to pour myself. Hers was half-full. I sat up and crossed my legs as if I was mature enough to handle the situation. "Whoa!" I commented as I let out alcohol-filled oxygen from my lungs. My maturity left, with the first sip. It was strong and very distasteful. "Hahahaa," she giggled at me with that unique laugh of hers. Auntie Pinkie talked and laughed through her nose, causing her to sing when she spoke and drag when she laughed. I found it charming, but I didn't know that her habits would have such an impact in my life and stick with me for the rest of my years. "My niece, do you want some soda pop in your drink?" "Yes Ma'am." She sweetened my next drink so that I didn't taste the liquor.

After a few more of those drinks, the mood opened up. We laughed, we cried and we bonded. I never knew this side of Auntie Pinkie. Well, that night I trusted her with my deepest pains. I released all those pains that had been decaying inside of me for years and years along with the new ones. She listened and took them with stride. She offered her advice, but she left it up to me. I wasn't an adult yet, but she assured me that all of the hell I had been through in my youthful age certified me as grown years ago. "Don't be mad at God for the life and the world He placed you in. Instead, be grateful that you're here and that you can begin a new journey because He allowed you to see. I love you, my niece." Her lesson stuck with me like warm oatmeal on a cold snowy day. We sealed the night with a big hug after finishing the big bottle of JB.

I plopped down on a beautiful canopy bed looking up at the sheer curtains spinning above my head. The next morning, I realized my head was the only thing that was twirling. I didn't have much of a hangover, which was a good thing, but my mind was still hanging on to the words that my Auntie Pinkie had spoken to me. As I swung back and forth between the episodes of my childhood, I wondered if she was the only person that knew about the hatred that Spivey had for me. I didn't understand why if people knew about how Spivey felt about me and if they thought something was wrong, why didn't they say anything? Auntie Pinkie's words about God and strength flashed through my mind, but I stopped in the middle of the confusion and let those thoughts flee from my mind…saving those mysteries for another time because I could use some greasy bacon with some sweet buttery grits.

I checked the pantry for grits, but found oatmeal. My stomach said, nope. I had to have some grits. Auntie Pinkie was awake and singing in the shower. "Good morning, my niece. How you feelin'?" she yelled over the splashing waters as if she had intruder sensors on the kitchen cabinets. I popped my head into the bathroom and said, "I'm good. I see you're fine too. I'm going to the store to get some grits. Do you need anything?" I asked. "No thank you. Grits sounds good," she said in a laughing voice. Seeing her happy that morning felt good, knowing that we had emptied that big bottle of booze the night before. That was certainly something I wasn't use to. "I'll be right back," I said as I grabbed the house key that she had given me.

Freedom at last, my soul sang as I strolled to the store. I said hello to the two Iranian men who were sitting outside the store on some blue crates while they fanned the flies and talked up religion. When I got inside, and walked down the aisle, I lifted my face up, and I smiled when I discovered the small box of Southern Style Grits. I wasn't sure that I'd find grits in that neighborhood, let alone Southern Style Grits. The clerk searched my eyes for familiarity. "Hi," I said in a warm voice. "Hello cutie. Did you just move around here?" he asked as he touched my hand and took the five-dollar bill. He winked as he handed me the change. I snatched it from his grip and left the store. I didn't bother to say good-bye to the two Iranian men sitting on crates outside, either. *"Apples don't fall far from the tree,"* I thought. I wouldn't be surprised if I turned around and found them checking out my butt. Whatever, I didn't care, my day was going along too good to be soaked up with politics right now.

Did everybody notice that I was a new face in the community? As the thought ran through my head, I saw a medium height brown-skinned young man approaching me. "I'm Devon. I live three houses down from Ms. Pinkie. She told me that her niece was going to be living with her and possibly going to school with me." Hi, I'm Shelby, nice to meet you." I shook his hand, as I perceived his lameness. I was too much for him. My adolescence had been ripped off. Devon still had his. He needed not shed his precious purity to the poison lurking within me. I could tell that my body and twitch intrigued him. Who knows how long he had been watching me. Probably, since the second I stepped out of the house. My private thoughts were interrupted when he asked, "would you like to hang out sometime, since you're new? I could show you around or whatever?" "Ah-yeah, I'd like that. It's cool," I replied. I took his number that he had already written on paper and walked back to the house.

"Hahahaa," Auntie Pinkie giggled as I opened the door. She had been spying on us from the Bae view window. I unpacked my sack, washed my hands and began to cook the food. I wondered what Auntie Pinkie was up to as it concerned me and possibly Devon. It didn't matter though, because I wasn't interested in Devon, but we could be neighborly. Anyway, the seasoning and the aroma hit the air, swung around the corner into the rest of the house and hung long after we were done eating. The scent hooked Jelly's nose too as he got out of his ride, he put some pep in his step. I fixed him a plate and he ate a good helping of what was left before he took my Auntie Pinkie out shopping. "Thanks Shelby, that hit the spot; I'm gonna need it messing around with your auntie and them stores." I laughed and locked the door behind them.

My nap was just that, a nap. It felt like I had been asleep for hours, but I had only been in a deep sleep for about twenty minutes before my own snoring woke me up. Good thing Auntie Pinkie cared. She said that my heavy snoring was a problem and that she was going to get me some help. I took a seat on the sofa, picked up the remote and the receiver then called Addison. "Where are you Bitch?" she shouted. "Stop calling me that,

Dating My Dad

please? I'm at my Auntie Pinkie's house. It's a long story, but I'll explain it later. What's going on in the hood?" I asked. Whatever it was, I was happy not to be there. Addison can be downright ignorant, (as my grandmother would say), sometimes. Addison was born screaming loud and knew everything. She didn't mean any harm, she got it honest, straight from her quarrelsome momma. "Where does she live, in the boonies somewhere?" "If you take the #2 bus, you can be here in about twenty minutes," I explained hoping that she'd come to visit soon. For once, I wanted to show off where I laid my head. Auntie Pinkie's house was tailor made for her, hell, every woman wanted a pampered paradise in the form of a house. Our conversation was cut short by a re-run of the Jefferson's in which Wheezy and George lied to Lionel and Jenny about taking their grandbaby to a modeling agency. I needed a laugh.

Anyway, the last time I had seen Addison began to invade my space, due to her trying to get information from me about that night. I had to get off the phone. I just didn't have the energy to recall that day sober and I didn't feel up to drinking. "Addie, can I call you back, I got to feed the dogs and walk them real quick?" I said. She approved and we got off the phone.

Sassy and Kingston were spoiled and boring. They ate human food and slept on the loveseat. They acted human too. My being in her spot irritated Sassy; I put a smile on my face and scooted over. She hopped up there and walked in a circle a few times, then laid down watching TV. Nothing excited Kingston except my aunt's arrival. He would wag his tail and start barking long before she was near the house. Sassy would join the bandwagon and start hollowing. They were weird, but I gave them their due respect. After all, I was the intruder. And, they were not my dogs, I didn't want to get too close and get my heart broken again.

Devon knew nothing of my horrible past. It was something I didn't share with him for my own personal reasons. Truthfully, I was ashamed and had pushed it back where it belonged, in the bowels of my constipated belly, near my rectum ready to release as soon as it softened. So what if it happened only a few short weeks ago, it was the olden days to me. My body held it and it simmered where only I could smell it. This is one reason I didn't bother bringing it back up, and I cringed at the thought of my history repeating itself. I can't blame Devon for not wanting to speak to me, but I didn't feel the need to volunteer and explain my pain to him, a stranger.

I didn't expect Kazeem to show up. How did he know where I was? All I could remember was Kazeem jumping out of the bushes screaming and swinging on Devon and me as we were on our way to the store. "What the fuck you doin' with my girl?" Kazeem yelled as he punched Devon in the face a few times. "Man I ain't her boyfriend, she's my neighbor!" Devon explained grabbing his eye. Kazeem couldn't hear Devon's answer for the jealousy blood pumping so loud through his swollen testicles. He looked like a large Rottweiler charging his opponent over a female dog in heat. I was speechless in a moment of denial; Kazeem wasn't himself, but Spivey in rare form. I was so scared that my words left me with the urine that fled my body. Devon took off running the opposite way. I was frozen stiff. I wanted to flee the scene too, but my feet stayed planted on the pavement until Kazeem dug me up from the ground. My legs dangled like roots as he shook me by the neck until I lost my breath. When I came to, I was in the ambulance sucking in oxygen coughing up blood. My heart skipped a couple of beats, but I wouldn't die. I wanted to. I needed to. Hell, I was a dead chick walking. Kazeem had killed my self-esteem and spunky spirit a long time ago. There was nothing left to take.

"Sweetie, what's your name?" a woman in white coat asked me. My wish had come true. I had died and gone to Heaven. Nope. The nurse raised the bed up to give me a drink. My throat felt like a damaged bridge and my tonsils were the broken levee sending a gushing flood of unwanted water into my body. "Shelby," faintly, I answered after swallowing. Auntie Pinkie and the police interrupted whatever else the nurse had to record. "Aaawh Baby are you okay?" Auntie Pinkie sobbed. She made me cry too. I was so happy that she was there. I was ready to get some stuff off my chest and I didn't mind opening up to her. She broke down the language of the investigator so I could understand. She helped me to fess up to the officers, accepting the help they offered. She knew that I was afraid to tell on Kazeem and ashamed that I was in the condition I was in.

After having a quick conversation with my aunt, I let them have it: his name and a full description of him. I told them everything that Kazeem was to me, all that he had done to me, even about the times he had pumped on me so hard that he caused me to be constipated for a week. I told them of the grown up things he made me do to him, where he lived and all his known hangouts and homeboys. I even told them of his obsession with Prince. In addition, how we had to enter the basement window like in the movie Purple Rain. I wanted him locked up for the captivity of my livelihood. They said if they caught him, I wouldn't have to appear in court because I was a minor, which made it all better. My bruised body and broken nose was enough witness to put him in jail for a long time. I had hoped the bars that surrounded him would resemble the mental prison he held me in. They informed me that Kazeem was a lot older than he said. He had fooled me and everybody else. He had flunked the fifth grade twice and didn't stay in school long enough to gain the credits needed to pass to tenth grade. Well, that explained his mature features. They also uncovered his thievery. He was wanted for breaking into his neighbors' homes and stealing everything he could carry.

Kazeem had another warrant for his arrest. It was for beating up some woman, could be the chick that woke me up cussing and throwing rocks through his basement window. She was using words I had never heard. It could've been Spanish. Whatever it was, I figured she was upset that I was there. When I asked him who was she, he said, "nobody!" They showed me a picture of her and asked, if I recognized her. I told them yes, but I didn't know her. Whoever she was, she had no front teeth in her mouth. Apparently, Kazeem was the villain who knocked them out. She dropped the charges, but the state had taken over the case and wanted his blood for all the violence he had done to her.

I was shocked. Kazeem had been living a double life. I would have never guessed that he was such a person who robbed and stole, cheated and beat up females. He was a mad man on a rampage. I replayed our encounters repeatedly in my mind, all the while thanking God for sparing me from Kazeem's wrath.

Episode 5

Dating My Dad

While visiting the old neighborhood, I felt as though I was in a Spike Lee movie; gliding through the memories and elevating myself past the pain that I had endured, when I lived there. The sun seemed brighter and warmer, the trees whispered sweet nothings in my ears as the green leaves touched and taunted my interest then manipulated my mind into the innocent essence of laughter that I once felt on those common grounds. I recalled the family, friends and familiar faces that filled the block parties and the gatherings that Spivey had out in the open field next door to our house, just because it was the weekend. Strangely, for a Saturday, no one was out. Maybe they were sleeping in or they were out doing the things they couldn't get done during the week.

I overflowed with bliss quickly from looking around my old stomping grounds. I glanced at my old garage, the one that I had played many childhood games in and around, the same one that I hid behind, whenever I ran from Spivey and his drunken outbursts. I remembered running to that garage for cover whenever it rained. If it hadn't been for that garage being so narrow, I probably wouldn't have been able to pass my driving test. I use to wait until Spivey went to sleep, then I'd steal his keys and be joy riding cross-town as if I was some big shot. That same garage also hid many of my unforgettable triggers. Zap! My gratifications left me, bombarding me with fear, dreadful memories of those moments of darkness when my purity ran from my body and headed for the hills of growing pains, a sugar-coated version of the harshest adversity I had ever faced.

The sound of some children playing caught my attention like a momma bird arriving with food for her young. I took off walking swiftly;

hopped the bus and went to see my mother. Regina was at work, as usual. I had made up my mind that I wasn't going to visit Spivey…and I didn't. I went on my way to a recommended group counseling session for girls who also experienced similar hurts. On the way there, I hoped for the best, I needed to clear my brain and collect the help that I wanted.

After listening in on a few stories, I was irritated. I mean, call me what you want, but I wasn't anything like the girls in there. I'm not saying they deserved what happened to them, but damn. They seemed to have set themselves up to attract the worse situations in life. Some of the girls had bad attitudes honestly; they looked forward to messy conditions. I didn't see myself like that. I saw myself as a fish that was swimming and had suddenly been swooped up. I got trapped in a mean net of lies, gestures, and manipulations from a hungry predator. In my mind, I had survived, after escaping through a tiny hole that scraped off my skin, almost to the bone, leaving my body dead, though my brain was still alive.

Not only was I disappointed, I was also disgusted. I couldn't relate nor fit in with the girls in the group session. The girls attempted to convince me that I was in denial. I begged to differ, their confessions led me to believe (wrong or right), that they came from the gutter and that they wanted to stay there. Many of them were trained and learned to pass out excuses for the men that raped and abused them, but I wasn't about to pardon Kazeem. Kazeem needed to pay for my life, the life he interrupted. Ain't no telling where I would have been mentally if I hadn't been a part of those sick plans that he had for me. One thing was for sure, I wouldn't have been there listening to those sob stories of how shit happens.

Why am I here? I asked myself as I stared at some chick with her baby's pacifier in her own mouth. It seemed as though we had been standing in line forever. I still wasn't ready even though I had been waiting since the sheriff called my number for me to come to the side counter to register. I showed him my fake identification and signed the slip stating that all the information I had given him was true. "Uhh sir, can-uhh-will the inmate get my personal information?" I asked with a lump in my throat. "No, this is for our records, only." I passed through the locked bullet-proof doors and allowed them to check me for any contraband. I took a seat on one of the many burgundy chairs, still trying to talk myself out of the unexpected meeting. Kazeem didn't ask for me to come and visit him, but I felt that I needed to see him face-to-face to tell him a thing or two. Especially since I knew that I was protected from him in a jail setting. There were bars, thick; bullet-proof plastic windows, surveillance cameras and guards with big guns, who only needed an excuse to pull the trigger. I rehearsed my entrance for a bit before they called my name. Fear of the unknown gripped me, seemingly, placing pauses in my steps as I moved forward to take a seat at a window. Nevertheless, I coached myself right into the seat in front of him.

Kazeem looked a mess. His hair was out of place, his lips were dry, as if he was withdrawing from drugs. He managed to crack a smile at the sight of me. I didn't return the kindness. I pierced his eyes with a glaze of "shooting silver bullets" straight through to his heart. I wanted him to feel my hatred for every ounce of pain that weighed heavily in my heart...and it hadn't depreciated. My anger had kept its value. My immediate assessment of him had justified my feelings and my annoyance with him as he seemed to be okay...he was still alive; just sitting there looking at him brought volumes of anger to my temperament. He grabbed the receiver to speak as he signaled for me to pick up the receiver hanging on the wall next to me. "Hello, I'm glad to see you Little One," he said with that smirk on his face. It was the same look that I had always hated seeing. I sensed a "click" and then a "shift" inside of me, and the boil over began. I exploded in his ear. Out came the rage that I had stored for him. My rapid fire of words sprayed in his ears as if leaving holes from a semi-automatic weapon. Bam! Bam! Bam! Bam! The shield echoed as Kazeem hit it with the receiver trying to stop me. He couldn't, and even though I still felt fear in my heart, I knew he couldn't touch me. Plus, I was mad as hell and didn't give a damn, at that point. I had mustered up the courage to go there and to see him face-to-face and he was going to hear me out, regardless of what he wanted. Even if the guards had not been around to see me, I wanted to prove to those chicks in my group meetings that I was a woman of my word and that I wasn't going to let him or no other man get away with abusing me. I wish I would make up an excuse for this sorry Son of a Bitch for hurting me!

"Ma'am? Calm down or this visit is over!" the guard warned me. I shut my mouth and eyed Kazeem down. I waited for him to say something. He sat there for a few minutes, then let out a loud evil laugh that seeped through the walls trying to shackle me down and bring me into his miserable prison with him. Thank God that Kazeem dropped the phone and rose up from his seat dismissing me. I sat there until I couldn't see the back of him anymore, then I exhaled. At that point, I had been relieved of the frustrations that I had suffered from knowing him.

Normally, I'd have a friendly conversation with a stranger on my bus rides, but I was distant and quiet all the way home. Yeah, I let him have it and got some anger off my chest, but I knew it wasn't over. I could still feel the other tank of suppressed bitterness leaking over into the one I had just emptied out on him. I recognized that I needed to talk to someone. I wanted to get rid of the cords of poison growing inside me.

Suicidal cravings crowded my thoughts as I waited for Auntie Pinkie to get home to comfort me. Thank God, she wasn't a pill taker and didn't have any medications around or else I would have given her a surprise when she arrived. Instead, I decided to drink myself into a "put it all on the table" confessional state whenever she arrived. I sucked the liquor out of the bottle of JB until I felt numb and happy. At that point, I was ready to tell it all.

It took her way too long to get home. I was half-dead of alcohol poisoning by the time Auntie Pinkie got to me. She raised my arm and it flopped down onto the bed. She didn't have to guess that I was drunk, I reeked badly from the empty liquor bottle, plus, I left more overflow evidence all over her toilet and sink. Auntie Pinkie didn't meddle with me. Once she confirmed that I would be okay; she let me sleep it off. "Child, you need some rest with all the hell you've been through," she sighed as she cut the lights off and left my door cracked.

The sun beamed hot on my face causing the sweat from my brow to slide into my closed eyes. The sizzle woke me up. I could've killed a cow with one mouthful of air. My breath smelled bad. I proceeded to the bathroom to brush my teeth, it was sparkling clean in there. The aroma of bacon and toast marched into my nostrils down through the maze and into my stomach. Suddenly, up came whatever hadn't made it out of me the night before. Yuk! The only thing there was coming out was greenish glob. I flushed the toilet and let down the lid. My Auntie Pinkie poked her head in to check on me. "You aah right?" she asked. I nodded as I continued to brush my teeth. I don't remember going near my tonsils, but I gagged and had to vomit again. Out came the same slime. "Auntie Pinkie!" I screamed. I was scared and unsure what was happening to me. "You got alcohol poisoning; let's get you to the hospital," she said. She grabbed her keys and a jacket for me and out the door we went as we headed to St. Mark's emergency room. It was obvious that the rich owned St Mark's, but mostly poor people went there because of its location. Years ago, the north side was predominately Jewish. But, as time went on, the area changed to Black, Puerto Rican and Asian residents. Nevertheless, St. Marks took care of those who needed help. They would not turn people away who were without insurance. Rumors floated that if you were near death, they would be the ones to bring you back to life without even thinking about it.

"If my complexion had been a bit lighter, my face would've turned blue after the nurse announced to me that I was pregnant and miscarrying. Good thing they couldn't convey that I had consumed the alcohol or I would have been in big trouble," I thought to myself. Maybe the alcohol was causing the miscarriage. Didn't matter, I was relieved to not have a child while I was still a child myself and plus by Kazeem.

The residue of the miscarriage incident lingered and hung around on our minds and in our conversations for days afterwards. Auntie Pinkie kept it between us, but we discussed it a lot. She recommended that I bring it to the table during my group counseling sessions for help.

Dating My Dad

Well, I took her advice and after the pity from the girls and counselors, I found myself back at the window visiting area with Kazeem. This time I didn't have a chip on my shoulder. I was led to talk to him about what had happened and to hear his feelings, it felt like the right thing to do until Kazeem went nuts. He beat the receiver against the window and spit at me. Globs of nasty looking saliva covered the thick glass. I was terrified. He had managed to make me feel his pain and bring me into the prison of his madness. I jumped up and ran for the exit.

The *"what did I do wrong"* song played repeatedly in my head for days. I know Kazeem loved me in his crazy kind of way, but I didn't know the news would hit him like it did. Auntie Pinkie said that he knew he had lost me and if I had the child, that baby would have been a guaranteed permanent connection with me. She said good thing he wasn't getting out for a long time. "Move on with your life Shelby," she advised. I wanted to move along, but I didn't know how. It seemed as if my life was damaged and the effects would last longer than welcomed.

Only a few months had gone by, but I will never forget that day of January 28, 1986. It was the same day that the Space Shuttle Exploded that I received an "I'm sorry card" from Kazeem. He must've gotten my address from the restraining order that I had against him. Kazeem's card came at an odd time, but for some great reason, I felt free. Free from the pain and suffering of being with him and out of the cage he had designed just for me. I felt free to do whatever my big heart desired, which was how I got the strength to go on and finish high school.

My graduation was the best ever. Spivey and Regina didn't come, but it didn't matter. Auntie Pinkie, Uncle Les and Addison were there and two of my three counselors came. Timmy, the police officer who arrested Kazeem, found it in his heart to sneak in and take a few pictures with me. "I'm so glad you made it Shelby. If I had a daughter, I'd want her to be like you. You are a survivor! Nothing can stop you, if you don't let it, little girl." Timmy spoke those words to me, causing my heart to jump for joy and cry at the same time. I believed him. I am a survivor and I did have it in me to do whatever I set out to do. I took those words of wisdom and applied them to my future. In order to set my path to success, I signed up and attended a couple of college night classes. I wanted to make sure that I could take care of myself, especially, since Spivey reminded me that, "I didn't take care of no grown people." Hell, he didn't take care of children either, especially me! Anyway, I took the quickest courses that would help me to get a decent job and earn a good salary, so that I wouldn't get put out anymore without a backup plan. Where most people have a plan A and B, I made up a plan A-Z. I could help Regina, if she wanted me to. I loved living with my Aunt Pinkie but she was single and had no kids, she didn't say it, but I knew she wanted her own space back. She'd let me stay with her forever, but I didn't want to wear out my welcome. I could never repay her for taking good care of me and I was surely grateful. Besides all of that, I dreamed of the day when I would turn 18-years-old. I dreamed that I was going to have a big house and a brand new car. Well, I soon learned that it wasn't possible unless my parents or somebody else that loved me enough and gave me a lot of money or left me an inheritance. I learned that in this world, if you want something, you have to go get it and you have to fight hard to get there. Anything is possible in America.

Episode 6

The doctor's words hit me like I had been kicked by a gigantic kangaroo in my side. She let me know that there was no need for a DNC because I miscarried early and there wasn't a trace of a fetus anywhere. It was as if I conceived one night and lost the baby the next. Unlike the last time I was pregnant, this time I didn't think much about it, it went in my ear and out of my body. I felt relieved and tranquil. Sure, I could run and tell Niko that I lost his child and he'd be all over me sad and helpless wanting to make another one, but I wasn't. I was happy to be on my way to the next challenge life had for me. Besides, I'll never forget what Auntie Pinkie told me about men getting women pregnant to keep them near and me knowing Niko the way I did, like Kazeem, I know he would use that as another good reason for us to stay together. Speaking of which, I have to ask Auntie Pinkie how to go about getting some birth control pills without health insurance.

I just don't see myself with him much longer; I've got to figure out a plan to get away from him. He's mean, controlling, all around abusive, lazy, a wannabe somebody else, trying to hang out with ghetto stars while pulling people in the gutter with him. He is a liar and hopefully a cheater; any excuse will do for me. Lately, I've weaned him from me, ignoring his calls, dodging his invitations. Hell, everything he asks of me, I make up an excuse and say no. Eventually, he'll get the point. Sometimes guilt drops by and tries to move in, but I politely tell it to take a hike, no vacancies!

Niko didn't love me as much as he needed me. When I introduced him to my family and Addison they all liked him at first and thought we were a cute couple, but once he got drunk, he changed right before their eyes and started talking that pimp talk and dancing like he was the coolest person that ever wore shoes. Though they liked to see him dance, they made sure to tell me the next day how I could do better. Addison called him a McDonald Pimp (she got that from Spivey).

Everyone only confirmed what I was thinking every time I gave him the benefit of the doubt and listened to his shattering promises of hope for a better future with him. Point blank, I just couldn't see myself with him too much longer, invading my upcoming advantages. I was young, disease-free and child-free. The world was mine and it needed to see me, not us. I refuse to let people see me making excuses for his abusive behaviors or explaining him not having a job. I wasn't brainwashed and it showed. I started turning the questions over to him whenever someone asked me something about him. I let him speak and stumble over his own reasons why he was unemployed, homeless, without a ride, bitter, mad and talked like he was a pimp with a stable full of silly women. I witnessed Regina account for Spivey's motives and he'd embarrass her even more. With Niko, I snatched that problem up from the roots and for that, he resented me. He wanted me to pamper him, baby him and be his yes woman, gofer girl and supermom but I wasn't. Hell would have to freeze over with the devil in it before I take care of a broke-ass man.

Regina and Spivey were sitting out on the porch playing Bid Wiz, ain't that odd, about time they learn to hang with each other. Regina had this two-faced grin on when she announced that we were moving again. "Down on Max and North Avenue," Spivey gladly let out.

"Are you for real Daddy?" I asked, hoping he was joking. "Why would I lie and who is you to lie to?" He returned, "Momma-uhh-never mind." "Never mind what Shelby?" Spivey interrupted. It has been a long time since he called me by my name. Anyway, I couldn't believe she let him talk her into moving on the Eastside and especially in the hood.

"What's wrong Shelby?" Regina asked with that funky grin on her face. She knew good and well what was bothering me, but since she wanted to push me, fine. I took a deep breath, wishing I had a cigarette. My right leg started to quiver.

"Well, we went over your income and we both agreed that we wanted better for all the hard work you and I put in. With both our incomes, we could afford to buy a new home, and a duplex. I could live in one and you and Daddy in the other, but we'd all be together."

"What the hell you mean we!" Spivey butted in. "You act like you're the man of the house and shit."

"Naw Daddy, it's better now that you are home and with all of our income together, we could split the mortgage down the middle and live well in a better neighborhood. Especially with you being disabled now you can get government help for us too." I knew he wasn't going to like that at all.

"We moving on the Eastside and that's that, hell. You don't run shit in no house of mine," Spivey said as he took a long drag from his cigarette and threw it to the ground. I turned to Regina for her input, but as usual she turned her head giving Spivey her attention. Fine! If that's the way she's going to be, she better not call on me when he's bashing her head in. And who's going to walk her to the bus stop to protect her, not Spivey. He'll be too hungover to be up that early to care about her well-being. I stayed a few more minutes, hearing Spivey rant and rave, then I excused myself into the house. "I ain't got time for this," I mumbled.

I didn't realize I had fallen asleep until Regina shook me, waking me up. "Shelby, I want to talk to you about something important."

"Okay, Momma," I answered as I rose up, wiping the cornbread crust from my eyes, and checking the clock radio for the time.

"You know your dad loves you a lot more than you think and a whole lot more than he shows," she smiled, "he's just old fashioned. He's trying to connect with you the best he can, you know?" "Momma, I'm grown and I'm his daughter, if we ain't connected yet, we ain't gonna connect at all." I answered rolling my eyes up into my head. She can keep on trying to feed me that mess if she wants to, but I wasn't eating it. I have had my full share of trying to mend things with him. He didn't approve of my opinion or my ideas. As I said, Spivey hated everything that had anything to do with me. If I knew that and accepted it, then why didn't Regina? She made me feel guilty for not wanting to get my feelings stepped on by him. Hell, I was tired, you get what you give and all he gave me was hell and a hard time. "Well, if he didn't understand you or didn't like you then he wouldn't have allowed Niko to come and stay with us." She said with a big smile on her face. I sat straight up in my bed. Who in the hell were they to barge in on my life like that? My emotions won the race with my brain trying to comprehend what my mother just hit me with.

"He what!" "Niko's going to be living with us," she smiled again. "Who said he could do that?"

"Your dad," she said as she looked surprised that I wasn't excited. Of all people, Regina knew I didn't care for Niko that much. She knew I was trying my best to get away from him. "Momma, don't you think y'all should've asked me first or seen how I felt about it?" I massaged my throat. It was lumpy and drying out at the same time, I was trying my best not to yell at her.

"Shelby, it'll work out, you'll see. Besides, your dad likes Niko. Y'all make a cute couple." Mad was an understatement for that moment. I could've emptied my penny bank, purchased a gun, walked up to Spivey and shot him, dropped the gun and went to sleep. As I said, he hated me; he would go out of his way to destroy me. I can't stand him. How is he going to know what I want if he don't know me? Regina said a few more words that sounded like screeching on a chalkboard to me and left my bedroom, pulling the curtain closed behind her. I plunked down on my bed and cried myself back to sleep.

The look in Niko's eyes said more than he let out of his mouth. He supervised me as I set up our room at the new house, making special adjustments for his needs. He needed the bed next to the window so he could crack it three inches for fresh crisp night air. The telephone had to be on his side so he could screen my calls. The TV had to be on my side because he slept on his right side up under me and could see better. He's lucky I don't kick his behind out, bossing me around like he's got a job paying all of our bills. For a moment, my mind drifted to the happiness of us living together and enjoying each other's company. But all of that was disturbed when he grabbed my butt and squeezed it as hard as he could. "Stop Niko! My parents are home and that don't feel good anyway." "I'ma be tearing this ass up." He put his big lips near my cheeks. "No you're not." "Look, I'm not going nowhere so you might as well get use to it. Hear me?" he planted on me. "I know Niko, I'm just saying chill out for my parents catch us." "Yo daddy 'nem know we going be fuckin, so stop tripping. They wouldn't have let me move in if they didn't want us to. Your dad told me he needed help keeping you in your place. And you know I'ma do that." He gave me a look as if I was his daughter and he was scolding me. He and Spivey can go to Hell.

"Niko, look I don't want to feel tied down. I got many things that I have to do. I signed up for school and I'm looking for a better job that's part time. I got my friends to go out with and I'm not trying to get tied up with no other responsibilities right now. You know?"

"I don't care what you do as long as you let me know where you are at all times and there ain't gone be no going out. You got a man now and we live together. You respect me, you understand?" He walked up on me and mean mugged me, pushing his finger into my forehead slinging my head back. I hated him! He wasn't my damn dad, but he sure did act like him.

"I hear you Niko. I'm going to respect you. I love you." I lied. I'd say anything to get his hands from around my neck and out of my face. Niko didn't have a full deck. He was obsessive and jealous. I mean I liked him, but when I saw him disrespect his mother and discovered he didn't want much out of life; I didn't want to waste my time with him. Could you blame me? This fool was 6 feet tall, stocky, with nothing to lose. Sure, good-looking on the outside with a smile that brightened everybody's day, but his eyes sent frightening chills down my spine whenever he wanted to get his point across. And that fact was, his way or no way at all when it came to a woman, especially his woman, me.

I came up with the bright idea of giving into Niko to keep the peace between my parents and us. Whatever he asked I did. At first, it was good, like the first night we made love. I came home from school; I took it that he was in a good mood. He and Spivey had been drinking earlier that day. This picture looked familiar, me working while he drank all day. Anyway, Niko had cleaned up the room and had it smelling like flowers. He had the lights dimmed and a glass of Pink Champale for me. He got in the bed, butt-naked under the covers and his private stood at attention. "Take your clothes off." He ordered; I didn't hesitate. I was in the mood for some of him anyway; I just never liked to approach him. I didn't want him thinking I wanted him at all, but my clothes fell off me like he had cut them off at the seams. Before I could finish sipping my Pink Champale, Niko had slipped his tongue between my legs twirling around my private area, causing me to tighten my grip on his head. "Shelby? You know that I love you. I don't do no shit like this and you are the first and only woman I'll ever do it to," I ignored him. "Okay," I responded, not knowing anything else to say. "Come here, lay on the bed," he coached. I turned on the arch of my foot and plopped down onto the soft bed. He continued to play with me in my area and before I knew it, he had me gripping the sheets. I forgot about my parents being there, my emotions snatched me into custody and I let go, giving into Niko's invitation to ecstasy. *"Damn, what are you stopping for?"* I asked myself, *"do me?"* I opened my eyes and found him standing over me staring at me with a hard-on. Hell no, I don't do that. "Okay," I agreed, knowing I couldn't, that was nasty. I talked about girls that I heard did that. And he thought I was going to stick him inside my mouth, he was crazy. I stalled as long as I could, trying to strike up a conversation; hoping he would be turned off and go to sleep. Instead, he asked me again with bass in his voice. I appreciate what he did to me, but I didn't ask him to do it and if he did it to get me to do it to him, that would be his problem, not mine. "Niko, I don't feel comfortable doing that. I ain't ever done it before," I gave. "I'll teach you. Just come on before I get sleepy." "I'd rather wait. Can we just make love?" "Shelby, stop acting like a two-year-old, we grown." "I know but." "What did I say Shelby, come on," his facial expression said he was angry. "No."

All I saw was blue and red lines. And when he had finished slapping me, he had a handful of my hair in his hand, trying to force my head into his groin area. I resisted, but his grip on my hair won. I grabbed his penis and put it in my mouth while tears rolled down my cheeks. I was mad as hell and wished I had the guts to bite him. After a few sucks he let my hair go and pushed me back onto the bed and forced himself inside me pumping me like he was teaching me a lesson. The whole ordeal was over before my hatred took root. Niko rolled off me and fell asleep, quickly snoring as if he had worked hard all day. I turned my concentration on his heavy breathing to keep myself from jumping out of the bed too soon to shower.

I scrubbed, scraped, and repeated my cleansing steps about five times before I felt clean enough to get out. I dried off, got dressed, called up Addison and left.

I stopped at the liquor store to cop a pint of vodka and bought some grapefruit juice on the way to Addison's house. Addison never seemed to have the right look on her face whenever I had something important to share with her so as usual I smiled; laughed, and joked with her about the good old days, eliminating my problems from my soul. I couldn't fool her though; she would pick at me sensing trouble, but I'd simply mention Spivey's name and she'd presume him to be the problem. I drank most of the Vodka, but I was glad she drank with me. They say misery loves company, what about confusion, which is how I felt most of the time. I always believed in treating a person the way I treated them so why was I receiving the drama. And why couldn't I be free? My Grandma told me a lot about being a woman and the challenges women faced and with that, she taught me to be free and independent. I wish she had taught me the laws of attraction, how I kept attracting knuckleheads.

I sat with Addison and her family a few hours enjoying being in their presence. Being around them always reminded me of my innocence with no worries. I asked Addison's mother if I could use the phone to call home. "Baby you ain't got to ask me no stupid questions. Local calls are free," she teased. Regina answered the phone in a cheerful tone. "Hey Momma, what are you doing?" "Nothing much, sitting up here with your dad watching Dallas. Where you at, Niko been looking for you?" "Is he there?" I really didn't care, but Regina didn't need to know something bad was going on between us. What would that be like, telling my mother that Niko slapped me because I wouldn't give him a blow job; too crazy for me. "Momma, can you get him to the phone please?" "Yeah, hold on a minute," she laid the phone down. "Who is that?" I heard Spivey ask. "Shelby," Regina said, "What she want?" "She wanna holler at Niko. Wait a minute honey?" "Niko?" I overheard. "Speak to me?" Niko asked picking up the other receiver. Who in the hell did he think he was? "It's me. Whats up? You up?" I swallowed the thickness in my throat. "Yeah, I've been up! Now get your mutherfucken ass here now!" He slammed the receiver down hanging up in my face. Regina must've heard him because I could still hear the TV downstairs going on. *"I was about to tell him that I*

Dating My Dad

was I on my way home, now he will just have to wait!" I thought to myself. "Gurly, I got to get ready to leave, this fool is tripping out," I announced to Addison. "Shelby, I heard him, he thinks he's your dad or something. I know you not gonna let that low-life tell you what to do?"

"Addison, I ignore him and you should do the same. I'm still here ain't I? He don't run shit, but his mouth." I finished my drink. I was scared of what was going to happen to me when I got home, but for now, I had the upper hand and that was that. We sat there reminiscing more and more. I hugged everyone goodbye and out the door and in my car, I went heading home.

I sat in the car for a few minutes finishing my cigarette before I entered the house. I kept an eye out for anybody coming out of the house. I wanted to pull off, but I didn't have anywhere else to go. It's a shame this fool had me scared to go into my own house. You would think he pays the bills or worse, we were married. But even if I were married to him, I still wouldn't want to come home to defend myself from somebody that is supposed to love me or someone I couldn't get rid of. *"Once I finish this cigarette, I'ma go in there, say hi to Regina and Spivey, fix me something to snack on, take a shower and get in the bed,"* I drilled to myself. At least I pray it'll go just that smooth.

Regina was in her bedroom with the door closed. Spivey and Niko were full of liquor; I could tell by the empty pints of gin sitting on the coffee table like dominos. The smell of alcohol lingered and hung thick in the air battling with the cigarette smoke. You would have thought you were in a badly vented bowling alley or a nightclub. Anyway, I spoke and kept straight to the kitchen. Spivey rose up and went into the bedroom.

Next thing I knew, Niko had me hemmed against the wall telling me what he was going to do to me as soon as we got upstairs to our room. I tried pulling away from him, but his grip was too tight. I wanted to slap him, but didn't want to cause a scene. "What's going on in there? Shelby you alright?" Spivey asked as if he was concerned. "Nothing Dad, I'm okay, Niko is just playing around with me." "Okay, let me know if you need me." "Okay," I responded. I reminded myself of how Regina defended him. This is messed up, he was disrespectful with a dose of paranoia.

Niko was caught up in his feelings about my whereabouts that he couldn't even wait until we got in the privacy of our room to start up with me; disrespectful bastard. "Niko let go of me please. I'll get to you when I get done. I wasn't doing anything but visiting my friends from the block and having a drink. What's wrong with you?" I spoke softly to him biting my tongue. "Get your ass upstairs now!" he said as he snatched my plate from my hand and threw it in the sink making a loud noise. My body shook. Fears and anger fought over territory inside me. Part of me wanted to grab one of Regina's pots and land it on top of his thick head and the other part of me wanted to scream for help. Either way, I didn't want to go upstairs with him. I was afraid of what he'd do to me or worse, what I'd do to him. I wish Spivey would have come in here and knocked the hell out of him and kicked him out on the curbside. "Okay, let me use the bathroom. I got to pee," I said as I put my hand between my legs holding it for sympathy. "Go ahead and bring your ass upstairs, I'll be waiting," he quickly responded. His eyes pierced straight through me like a dart. He felt it in his gut that I was stalling, and I was.

I stalled as long as I could. I took my precious time taking inventory of things we needed for the bathroom while washing my hands. I looked in the mirror to memorize my facial features. I should've just stayed home and I wouldn't have to go through this. I'm a grown woman! I don't have to answer to no damn body! I pulled the door open slowly and stuck my head out checking for that fool. My senses told me he was near and angry with me for taking so long. I took a few steps forward toward the stairs. Flashbacks of me running out of the door in fear of Spivey's beatings crossed my mind and my body froze. I fought the frost to keep walking toward the stairs leading to my room. I wanted to grab that doorknob, twist and run free, but the woman in me screamed, "Don't be afraid of that fool!"

She lost because I ended up sitting on the bed pleading for Niko to forgive me for not reporting to him while he choked the air out of me. "Baby, I won't do that no more, I promise," he said. I made myself sick, begging this fool for my life like he owned me. Finally, he released his hands from around my neck. "Shelby, I love you, but you bring out the worst in me because you don't listen to what I tell you. You're hard-headed as shit," he scolded. "I'ma listen to you I promise Niko. You just think I'ma leave you and go be with someone else, but I'm not. I'ma be right here. I promise." "Don't promise me shit just watch yo self for you get hurt." The look on his face told me he was dead serious. "What the fuck you rolling your eyes for?" he asked. He reached for me, but I jumped back and he missed me. "I didn't roll my eyes Baby." I lied, I didn't know he saw me. The way he walked toward the dresser, I thought he was getting his shorts to go to bed. He tricked me and open hand back-slapped me. My head bounced against the wall. My heart leaped out of my chest. I tried to scream. but he slapped me again shutting me up. We tussled and tussled with each other before falling onto the bed. Somehow, he got a grip on my neck again pressing on my collarbone with his arms. I relaxed my body surrendering. I just wanted it to stop. "Don't make me do this Shelby. Take your clothes off now!" He was a lunatic. "Hey, what's going on in there?" Spivey asked through the door. "Nothing man, we alright," Niko answered. "A man I need y'all to keep it down in there so my wife can get some sleep. Y'all hear me?" "Sorry Dad," I reassured. "Don't be sorry keep it down." He left. I began undressing, Niko followed. I cut the lights off and slid into bed under the covers, Niko followed. He brushed his heavy hands over my body like he was wiping down a car. He had the nerve to ask me to get on top of him. "I don't want to Niko, my face hurts and my arms are sore." "Can I get some head then?" "Some what?" No the hell he didn't ask me no crap like that. He wasn't a king and even if he was, I wasn't putting my mouth on his nasty body nowhere. "My mouth hurts. Can we just lay next to each other and get some tomorrow? I'm calling in sick in the morning. I knew I had a bruise on my face and I didn't want people to see me that way." I hope he feels bad for messing my face up. "You must've been fucking somebody with yo lying ass. You wasn't over no damn Addison's house Bitch," he mumbled, turning his back to my face. My heart pounded and sweat seeped from my pores. You the Bitch, I mumbled and got out of bed and hunted for my slippers underneath my bed. I grabbed my robe, slipped it on and closed the door behind me headed to the family room.

    I flipped through 250 channels at least four times before discovering a good scene in a movie. I didn't get to catch the name of it, but whoever she was, she had been abused too many times by her husband. She had removed the kids from the home one by one, then set the house on fire with her husband sleep or dead in the bed. If Regina and Spivey wasn't home and I had the courage and could get away with it, Niko wouldn't make it to see tomorrow because I got a few boxes of matches and some charcoal fluid. Truth be told, he wasn't worth me going to jail for most of my life or the rest of my life. But I promise, first thing in the morning I'm going to get a Restraining Order on that fool and get rid of him, for the last time. Who in the hell does he think he is threatening me in my own house, especially while my parents were there?

Of all the people I could've seen, I spotted Niko's mother at the courthouse. I hid behind the Nelson's Shoe Shine studio. I didn't want to explain why my face was bruised to someone who knows it was a strong possibility that her no good son had 99.9 percent to do with. I waited until I didn't see her anymore and took off toward the staircases to the Department of Family Violence.

The intake specialist was rude and numb. Maybe she had seen and heard it all before, but she didn't know me from a hill of beans and I would appreciate it if she would've stopped popping that damn gum while asking me questions. "Do he live with you? Because if he does, we need another address to serve him." Pop! Pop! Pop! She went on with her gum, so I hopped up and excused myself. "I'll be right back. I have to use the restroom." I lied. Today was just not the day to be fooling with this mess. She saw the bruises on my face, what more stupid questions did she need to ask of me? She acts like I was lying to her or something. Everything in me wanted to turn around and report her to her supervisor. I done took off work and put my last few dollars in the tank to get down here. It took me forty minutes to get a decent parking space. I'm not making any money because I don't have any more sick days at work. Pissed off was too kind of a word, I was hot and furious. Probably hot enough to go home and start up with Niko by talking about what he did to my face, then calling the police on him and have him arrested in the act. I'll find another way to get rid of him. I hoped that the ride home would calm my nerves.

Episode 7

Two months later

I can't take it anymore! Ever since Niko has been living here, he's been smothering me. I mean all over me. Where you going, who you talking to on the phone, why you wearing those clothes, and why you got to do it like that, do it like this? I mean just all in my way, telling me what to do like he's my dad or a drill sergeant of my one-woman army. I can't use the restroom without him being right there to smell it. And the sex, way too much! I don't like having sex five and six times a day. Damn, I do like to clean my behind in between sessions. I don't even like having it with him knowing he wants it just to see if I've been faithful to him. I mean, goodness, who, what and where could I get some so soon within the 30 seconds it took me to get to the store and the 30 seconds it takes me to get right back home. I don't go anywhere without him dragging along complaining about everything I do, trying to sabotage my flow. Of course, he still hasn't found a job and the piece of car his uncle gave him took its last breath after we put it on the highway to blow it out. His uncle lied, saying that all it needed was a good long drive because it had been sitting up. Once we got that car to another mechanic, he said the car was nothing but a shell, underneath had rusted away.

Anything that I want to do, Niko has to do so he hops in the car with me tagging along. He's tried a few times to drop me off at work and keep my car, but I wasn't having that. Hell, he didn't have any money for gas or repairs if something went wrong. Hell no, he wasn't getting my car. I wished he would've taken any job to handle his own business. I felt like I had a toddler transporting him around without a car seat. I wasn't his momma and didn't want to be. Outsiders' egged him on by saying how cute of a couple we are and how we're always together and some strangers (women) say they wished their men would hang with them like Niko hangs with me. If only they knew what I went through being with somebody like him, headaches, headaches and more headaches. I've always dreamed of a man that was self-sufficient, an enterprising person and strong, not this excuse of a man that mistreats me on top of all of the other things wrong he does. Spivey didn't make things any better, he and Niko hung tight all day, everyday drinking and messing up the house while Regina and I worked and cleaned up after them. Regina didn't seem to mind one bit, but I did. I must have been giving into the mundane lifestyle that I've witnessed all my life?

"Just Got Paid" by Johnny Kemp was pumping through my radio speakers on my way home. I was snapping my fingers and dancing in my seat as I headed up to 27th Street. I tooted my horn at the chick in the car next to me because she was dancing and hopping around in her seat too like we were listening to the same jam. I love listening to Renegade on the 5 o'clock Mix. I mean, he mixed jam after jam for that whole hour. Then they announced he was going to be spinning records at Persons Lounge and I didn't give a damn what Niko had to say, I was going.

I swung a left on 76th Street and headed to the Burt's Boutique for some bad threads that would make a man's mouth water when I walk in the door. I loved to shop there, everything was exclusive and he only carried one size, my size. I spent a little more than I would at any other women's clothing store, but who cared I didn't have to worry about seeing no other tramp in my outfit. I left there and went to Baker's to get me some sharp shoes and a bag to match. I damn near spent all my money. Hell, it had been so long since I spent my own check on me, I didn't know how to act. I felt free and happy.

I was just about done dressing when Regina and I heard the front door open. It was Spivey and Niko and they were sloppy drunk and all over each other. Niko was hanging over Spivey's shoulder with his right hand in Spivey's left hand. I heard Niko ask for me then I heard a thump on the floor. Spivey dropped him, "Shit this fool heavy. Hey honey. I took him to the Grapevine for some drinks. They bought us all kinds of drinks. Every time I go in there they always ask where that little girl at." *"I got a name, bastard,"* I said to myself. Spivey's speech slurred as he talked to Regina. You would've thought he was guilty or something the way he acted all apologetic and submissive. Regina soaked it up like a dry rag. I rolled my eyes and kept on getting dressed, putting on my last eyelash and curled them up. I turned and looked at Regina as if she were my mirror. I could see in her eyes that I reminded her of how she use to look getting all dolled up to go out.

At times, I look at her and see what could be my future, I hope my youthful looks don't get stolen like hers have; from her bruised up life. Sometimes when I look at her, I get scared, afraid that I'm not strong enough for the both of us to pull her out of the rut she's been in for the past nineteen years. Regina degraded herself to boost Spivey's shallow ego, when she use to be the sharpest thing walking the streets. Now she covers up her shine with her long hair in her face and oversized clothes. As I said, Spivey succeeded in transforming her outside to match his disgusting insides.

Anyway, I wish she and I could go out on the town together and have a blast as mother and daughter, hanging like sisters. I would ask her to come out with me if she wasn't caught up in the web Spivey spun around her mind all those years. She wouldn't know what it would be like to burn free and have fun. Any trusted prolonged negative force can pull you into a direction you would've never thought of going and you may never be able to turn back from. Well, I'm going to keep on hoping and standing in the gap waiting to usher her into the peace and joy that she deserves whenever she's willing to jump out and grab it. I kissed Regina on the forehead and told her to sleep well and I left out of the door.

My ID didn't look a thing like me and Addison didn't look 28-years-old, but Scooter let us right in. Us having on those high cut shorts, tank tops and hoe-boots up our legs could've been the password. Scooter grew up with us. He admired the cuties we turned out to be instead of the tomboys he use to know. He knew we weren't going to cause any trouble; we were big spenders' magnets. As soon as we walked in the door, all eyes were on us. Renegade gave us recognition over the MIC. We waved back like some ghetto celebrities and searched the darkness for some seats.

This tall skinny decent looking man greeted us. He introduced himself as Lovely with a smile so bright that made you smile back at him. His skin was very dark and smooth, but his hands were rough as I shuck them. "What you drinking Red?" he called me with that smile on his face. "My name is Shelby." I took my seat opposite of Addison. "Well, you look like a delicious red apple with caramel on top." I admit I was looking very sexy in my red boots and outfit to match. Truthfully, I looked like a street-walker. No wonder Lovely approached me. From what I heard about him, he use to be the biggest pimp Milwaukee has ever seen came through there. If he was looking for some money makers, we ain't the ones. "I'm

Addie and you, who the hell are you?" I overheard Addison say to Lovely's friend. "Kilo's my name getting money is my game." Addison turned up her nose. I kicked her leg under the table. Back then a lot of men called themselves Kilo because they indulged in illegal drug slanging. I wasn't going to get beat up or kidnapped by these fools because of her sassy mouth. Thank goodness, she turned him on. "I'll give anyone of y'all fifty dollars to let me see the hairs on your cat," Kilo laughed as he pulled out a crisp fifty-dollar bill. I looked over at Lovely while he sniggled at the question, but waited to see our response. "Fuck you ya black bastard!" Addison barked. I stood up and pulled my shorts to the side and Lovely and Kilo leaned forward until they could see my red hairs. "Damn, you got the right one baby," Kilo giggled to Lovely and dropped the 50 dollars on the table. I stuck my hand in the crotch of my shorts, then slid them back in place, snatched my money and sat down.

Lovely eased into the booth next to me and kissed me on the cheek. "Where you get them red hairs Red?" "I get 'em from my Momma," I said as I smiled. Part of me wanted to be embarrassed, but the rest of me said, what the hell. They didn't know me and I didn't care one bit I was 50 dollars richer. Addison rolled her big eyes at me. I rolled mine back. If only she knew, I was so happy to be out with her, able to be myself, ain't no telling what I was going to get her into tonight.

"You know what, I like you Red and it ain't because you showed me those red hairs. You remind me of my jeep." We both had to laugh at that one. "Naw, but seriously, I use to keep an eye on women like you for management purposes before, but I can tell you different." "Is that so?" I took a sip from my drink. "What else you want to drink?" he asked.

"Another Sloe Gin on the rocks?" I was feeling it and ready to dance, but Lovely was blocking my action. His breath was a bit tart, nope, it was hot and tart, like he hadn't been to the dentist in a while, but I took it like a woman. The last thing I wanted to do was to make him mad. I did offer him a breath mint though.

"Damn Red, I'd rather clothed you than feed you! For you to be so little, you can put it down." I paid Lovely no attention. I just kept on stuffing my face with those big fat ass expensive shrimp that he was paying for in the end. "Man, she too little to be eating like that," Kilo added. I didn't care for a salad, I loved to eat, especially when someone else was paying. And if Lovely thought this meal would get him in my panties, he had better think again, because I know whom I had to go home to. However, I was going to keep his phone number, his demeanor intrigued me.

Addison sipped on her Sprite and ate her huge slice of cheesecake. "I wonder if you're as sweet as your sweet-tooth, Ms. Addie," Lovely flirted. I wanted to slap the smile off his face. Thank God Addison and I were tight like a pair of vise grips and on one squad because he just kept on picking with her though she was being silent. "What's it to you!" Addison let out and that was the last thing I heard before the plate went crashing to the floor. "Okay, let's get out of here. Lovely, I enjoyed myself, but we have to get going now, it's late." I looked over at Addison and we took off towards the restroom to clean and leave. I knew she was upset because Kilo was old (35-years-old), but his money was young and I wanted her to participate, so I could use her for an alibi to keep seeing Lovely, but first thing's first, Addison was my friend and she comes before anybody so it was time to go and that's what we did. I'd explain it to her later how to take that candy from that baby Kilo on the way home.

I took it that Addison was glad to get home, she didn't even say good night or how good of a time she had. She opened the door and said, "see ya," shut the door and proceeded to her front porch. I was too full and happy to care. I pulled the lever back to D and smashed off.

I was exhausted and ready to get in my bed. If Niko said anything to me tonight about my whereabouts, I was going to let him have it. I had a great time and was looking forward to much more fun-filled nights without him and with Lovely. I saw smoke as I pulled up on our block and fire the closer I got to our house. "Oh my God!" It was my house on fire! My mind had a billion and one thoughts running around trying to find something to say or do. I damn near left the car in drive when I hopped out and ran to the front. Regina was pacing in circles in front of the house. Spivey was mad and cussing out any and everybody until he spotted me. "Bitch this is all your fault, that mutherfucken piece of shit man of yours, ole jealous ass fool. I hate him and bet not see his ass no more around here else I'ma kill 'em. You hear me Bitch!" he hocked up mucus like he was hacking up a lung and spit on the ground so hard I thought he left a print.

I sobered up quick after that. I took a step back out of Spivey's way; I wasn't sure what he was going to do. He just looked mean and ready to blow up and punch somebody. If he hit me, I'ma knock the hell out of him. Like a puppy, Regina ran up behind him. I sat down on the curb wondering what happened and where could Niko be. It would be better for the laws to catch him than for Spivey to get a hold to him. I stalled for a moment, holding myself. I had to use it and use it badly. I walked over and stood behind Regina poking her in her side for her attention. "What!" she snapped. "I have to use the bathroom Momma. Will you come with me to the Tommy's Fish Kitchen so I can go to the bathroom?" I plead. "Honey, I'll be right back. I'ma go use the restroom," she informed Spivey. "I'll be here watching our shit burn up and get watered down by these hopeless careless ass firemen." He looked pass Regina at me, I turned my head.

"Momma what happened?" I asked as I squatted over the toilet. While blow-drying her hands Regina responded, "Shelby, that Niko is something else. When he woke up and saw that you weren't there, he searched the house and caught a bad attitude. It was contagious too cause your dad watched how he opened the refrigerator and slammed the door. Then your dad started mumbling saying how he don't pay no rent and stuff, but he goes in and out our refrigerator like he put some food in there and the next thing I know they were going at it." I flushed, cleaned my hands and hurried up over to her to hear the rest of the story; my stomach bubbled as Regina told me how they had torn up the house fighting and carrying on. "Momma all this happened because Niko was mad because I wasn't at home?" "Yes." "Momma I'm sorry, but it wasn't my idea that he lived with us at all." I wiped my hand on my shirt. "Yeah, it wasn't your idea, but you didn't stop us from letting him stay even after he was beating on you!" "He don't beat me Momma!" I denied. "Shelby you can't add fabric softener to clothes that are already dry. I know what's been going on. And you allowed it so that's why he did it." She had her nerve. I knew Regina was right, but what upset me was she knew and said nothing until now.

The property owner didn't have homeowners insurance and offered nothing but a threat toward Regina and Spivey for burning up his house.

"Hit the road Bitch and go find that loser of a man of yours and stay with him!" Spivey's words circled my brain confusing me as I stood there listening to him. I know he was mad, but it wasn't my fault, I was mad too. Did he forget he was the one who went over my head and invited the psycho to our home to stay?

We lost everything we had in the fire except the clothes on our backs and the shoes on our feet. We split up. Regina and Spivey moved in with one of Spivey's drinking buddy named Carl. I went to stay with Addison and her family. Deep down inside, I was glad of the split, I was tired of living in chaos anyway. With Spivey and Niko together, I was bound for the nut-house at any time. I called a few times; they didn't have any beds ready.

Episode 8

I have learnt that a girl can get all the personal awareness, advice, guidance and support a home girl can give, yet still be manipulated and persuaded to fall in love with a perpetrator. As for me, I wish men came with labels like a pack of cigarettes warning you of what lies ahead. Because if I had one clue that Bishop Styles would turn my life upside down, inside out, I would have spit in his face the day I met him, approaching me with that weak line of, "can I take you by the hand and lead you to my heart so you can hold it?" Like I said, I would've went deep within my belly and spit up into his face and complained to the Surgeon General about the misprint, hell, an all-out false advertisement. I would have sued the hell out of them too. His label should've read; <u>Ladies of Milwaukee and all around the world</u>! <u>BEWARE OF THE B.S.</u>! If I just had a nickel for every time Mr. Styles pulled one of his stunts on me, I wouldn't have enough room to hold all of the money.

In the beginning of our courtship, Bishop came off as adventurous, charming, smart, and very open-minded. I dug the way he pronounced all of his words properly without any profanity. He even challenged me to read more to build my vocabulary. "Reading will give you wings," he'd encourage. Physically, I wasn't attracted to Bishop, I was impressed by the way he handled himself. He was light skinned, knock kneed and round, older and wiser, different and unique in his own way. Though he was corny, he wasn't a follower at all. I felt a little intimidated. He had lived in various places around the world, places that I had not ever been blessed to enter, which always made way for him to be the guest speaker in most of our conversations. I hadn't ever been outside the borders of Wisconsin; what did I know? He had been in the military most of his life and for whatever reason, he came back home to Milwaukee to raise those cute little green-eyed, red-headed twin boys, Tony and Terry. They were adorable to me. They were well-mannered and a delight to be around. They all tugged on my heart, treating me like a queen.

Bishop shared with me that about a few years back, their mother ran off with another soldier on base and left him with the boys and he didn't know where she was. He also said the boys hadn't seen or heard from her since they were two-years-old. That got to me. How could a mother leave her kids like that and for a man? I actually caught an attitude with her, a woman I didn't even know. After getting to know Bishop a bit more, I felt the need to not only open my mind thinking outside of my little box, but also open my heart. The relationship just felt right. I couldn't let my past bad experiences with men shut me down. I trusted Bishop; he was not the typical low-life, just a good man done cold by a cold-hearted crazy ass woman. At first I was ashamed, but I decided to tell Bishop all about my painful childhood living with Spivey and of course the abusive relationships with Kazeem and Niko, I mean I let it all out, every little detail as we sat in the park. I could barely hold back my tears. "You've been through a lot for somebody your age. But you don't have to hurt anymore. I am here and I am not going anywhere," he assured. I lay in his arms crying and wiping my face. I believed him and hugged him even tighter.

Before I knew it, time passed easily. Bishop, the boys and I were spending more and more time together doing new things. Like, going for long drives to nearby states visiting some of the most beautiful zoos I had ever seen. I'd stared out of the window site seeing, excited to be going to new, unfamiliar places. The boys seemed to be use to it all, it was obvious that I wasn't. I wasn't use to doing anything family-oriented. I could only recall wishful thinking of days as such.

 Anyway, we were getting closer and closer by the days, squeezing out any and everything that didn't fit. I didn't even have time for my best friend Addison, whom I haven't had the decency to call and tell her about Bishop and the boys. I'd have to find the time one day. However, we were growing close, so close that it caused others to envy us. Speaking of which, his mother made it her business to stay up late one night waiting for Bishop to let him know that I wasn't the twins' mother and she didn't appreciate me forcing myself on them. "Are you serious?" I asked. I was mad as hell and split seconds away from hanging up the phone, jumping in my car driving right over there and bursting through her giant Bae window and rolling out on her like G.I. Jane. "She said that you are ghetto and I need to be careful of whom I have around the boys influencing them, but I didn't pay her any attention. I just need to get my own place and get up out of her house with her damn rules. I don't know why I let her convince me into moving in with her from the start." Bishop tried to explain. "I don't give a damn! Your mother don't know me. I ain't told the twins to call me momma. They started that on their own and I never told them not to. What's wrong with her?" I jumped in. The fool in me started battling with the good angel on my shoulder; I wanted to yank the stick out of her butt for putting her uppity nose in our business. "Bishop I love you and the boys, but your mother is too damn snobbish for me. She criticizes any and everyone that's not on her level, in her rich neighborhood. But she ain't got to worry about me coming over there anymore. And I told you that she didn't like me!" "What are you yelling at me for? I'm just telling you what she said," he said as if I was the one wrong. I was mad and I felt threatened of losing what I thought was the best man and life I'd ever had at the time. It's either her or me.

I guess I won, a month later, Bishop and the twins and I were in our East side huge three-bedroom house, just in time for me to get the boys enrolled for the first day of school. Bishop had to go job hunting so he signed the papers giving me temporary guardianship so that I could enroll them. I felt like Diana Ross stepping out on the stage as I walked through the halls with the twins. Tony was a bit nervous, but Terry was all for it and eyeing down little girls. "Can I help you Ma'am?" the nice secretary asked me. "We just moved in the neighborhood, I heard this was a great school and want to enroll my boys," she smiled at the compliment and hurried to check the computer for openings. She brought her head up with a smile and I returned a grin. The twins looked up at me and I leaned over to kiss those orange cheeks of theirs. "We would love to have these two handsome young men join us and guess what? They will be in the same classroom." She smiled again. I looked away at the students walking by and asked; "is it possible that they can be separated?" To me they were individuals and I wanted them to be treated as such. "Let's see?" She put her head down again and glared through the list. Up she came again with a smile, "Yep, we can accommodate you." "Yeah," I was excited.

I stayed up at Eastland Street School all day with the twins, meeting the teachers, students, and the principal, seeing just what the school had to offer us. I got some weird looks for being twenty-years-young and having 6-year-old twins. It wasn't their business, it was the twentieth century and

Apple Dailey

families came in all kinds of ways. I ignored them and kept on digging for the good they had to offer their students. By the time I was ready to leave the boys were walking down the hall ready to go home, so home we went.

I whipped up some chicken and macaroni casserole and a jug of grape Kool-Aide. I had gotten full from taste testing. I put a plate up for Bishop; the boys loved it and ate the rest. They washed their hands and asked if they could go outside. "No, your rooms still have to be straightened up and I know you each have a worksheet to finish for school. "Oh yeah Momma, you have to fill out this slip, we're going on a trip to the pumpkin farm in a few weeks." Terry interrupted with his proper speaking self. "Me too Ma," Tony included. For them to be identical twins they acted so different, but I like it, it was easy for me to tell who was who. Tony must have his mother's eyes; they were much wider than Terry's or was Terry just sneaky. Even more, I love them the same, how could I not love well-mannered respectful and loving children. I just thank God that I didn't have to mess up my body bringing them into the world. Anyway, we got along just fine, so what if I wasn't their biological mother, I cared for them as if I went through the hard labor to bring them here.

Bishop burst through the door with a big smile on his face. I thought he was going to tell me he found a job. Instead, he grabbed me around my waist embracing me from behind. "Shelby, I'm the luckiest man in Milwaukee," he said as he kissed me on the back of my neck. "Yeah, why is that?" I raised my eyebrow trying to figure out what was up. "I'm happy to have my boys and you. I feel like a king and you know what I didn't have any luck today, but I made the decision that you're not going to work outside the home, if that's okay with you?" His eyes looked so sincere,

Dating My Dad

that sounded good and all, but, I wasn't raised that way. "Okay, but how? We need to pay these bills and the boys need things and..." "Don't worry about all of that Baby, I got us." He interrupted and simply stated, "It won't be long before I get to working and I'll make no less than fifty grand a year. You can go back to school or work part time if you choose." I hugged Bishop so tight. He loved me and thought the world of me. He just wanted to take care of me. Never can I remember being given the opportunity to choose. Moreover, neither do I remember Regina having the choice. I was always told what to do or something was forced on me or demanded of me. I loved him so and never had I been so sure of a man. "Okay honey, I'm going downtown tomorrow to see a guidance counselor and see what they have to offer for classes and see if I can get in soon." I placed his warm plate of food before him with a hand towel and drink then left the room to get the phone book. Terry and Tony were out front playing football. I smiled at them and giggled inside, life was perfect.

My heart was happy, pumping healthy blood throughout me transferring an army of chills over my body. I was excited about being able to go back to school for something I really wanted to do. I liked being a Certified Nursing Assistant (C.N.A.), but they were in the process of firing me, I could feel it in my bones. They were understaffed expecting me to get fifteen people cleaned up and dressed in the three and a half hours they gave us. They taught us in orientation not to take shortcuts, so I didn't. If a patient could walk, I let them walk. I felt that any bit of independence helped them. Besides, I may live long enough to need that kind of help. Truth be told, I had a conscious, I couldn't mistreat people because I could get away with it. Which is why I didn't understand why I continued getting written up for stupid stuff. Hell, it took me at least an hour to get myself dressed without make up. It didn't matter, with Bishop's support I was going to take advantage of the offer and do something better with myself.

The sun outsmarted me, it was shining bright through the windows inside, but the air was crisp once I opened the doors. It was chilly, causing me to give myself a big hug as I stood outside waiting. Bishop and the boys pulled up just in time, picking me up from orientation for school. It was good to see their smiling faces. I waved and smiled back, "Hey Ma." Tony yelled out the window, "Hello Momma." Terry greeted as I got inside. Bishop gave me a soft thigh rub and planted a moist kiss on my cheek. "Tell me about your day?" he followed. I appreciated that about Bishop, he always wanted to know how my day went and how I was feeling. Surprisingly, he didn't rush me into a sexual encounter with him. I wasn't the finest girl in Milwaukee, but I was for sure the sexiest. I filled out pretty nice and ripe over the years. I imagined it came from having sex at a young age. Anyway, I never felt rushed with Bishop by no means. In my eyes, he's what I consider a good man and a patient one too. "Well, they found me something I like to do. I passed the test and I got the financial aid rolling. I won't have to go that long. I start next month." I smiled. "Oh yeah, what did you decide on?" I hesitated. "Aah, an electrician, a Journeyman," my eyes squinted. "Why that?" I detected an attitude. "A-ah, because once they showed me what they did, I liked it and you said to go for something I liked, right?" "Yeah, but Shelby that's a little rough isn't it?" "Not really, they showed me what it takes to become a Journeyman Electrician and I can do it. I'm aware that electrical shock is a common factor, but tomorrow isn't promised to any of us, nor how we go out, but we all gotta go one day?" I pursed my lips. Bishop threw the gear in "D" and dashed off as if he was upset. He could be an ass sometimes, but not a total ass. I know he was older and all, but, I was grown and capable of making good decisions when it comes to my future career. It was the right men that I had a hard time choosing, not my career. Therefore, I had to take care of me the best I could.

The house was clean, the boys were asleep and I showered and got myself ready for bed. As I walked toward the stairs, anticipation stopped me in my tracks. I skipped over to the living room, grabbed my book bag, and headed towards the kitchen. I couldn't wait to see what I would be studying first. I was excited about becoming an electrician and making my own money and plenty of it. I would be able to take care of myself well, and help Regina out. I wouldn't have to depend on anyone for nothing. With the bread that Bishop will be bringing in, we'll clean house and I'd be able to get me a fancy foreign ride like the one he had. I appreciated him and his accomplishments, but I deserved my own too. I wanted to travel around the world as well, maybe with him and the boys, but if not, I was willing to gain my own adventures, not just hear about everyone else's.

Bishop crept up on me and asked, "Baby you coming to bed. You have to get up early for work tomorrow. And you know how cranky you are in the mornings." I didn't know he would say that about me without acknowledging his part in it. I was cranky in the mornings because he would wake me up at dawn like a damn drill-sergeant. "I'm coming Bae, I just wanted to go over this syllabus right fast. I'll be up. I'm geeked up."

"Okay, but don't say I didn't warn you," he said to me as he took a few steps toward the stairs. I stopped him and asked, "Bae, are you happy for me?" I just had to know. My gut feelings gripped me, holding my attention, and forced me to beware. "Sure, but why do you ask Baby?" "Because…" I smiled and ducked my head back into the flimsy book. "I'll be upstairs waiting for you to cuddle with me." He blew me a kiss. I caught it and ducked my head back into the book. I read a couple more words and put all the books back into my bag. I'll call Regina tomorrow and give her the good news.

"Hey Bae, I didn't ask you how your day was. How was your day? Did you find anything today or hear anything?" I asked, as I got into bed. He gave me the creeps staring at me without a word said, "I'll talk to you about it in the morning, I'm sleepy Baby." He approached me for some loving. "You're right Bae it is late. I'm not telling you no, but I got to get some sleep." I am in charge when it comes to my body, not him. "Good night," I said as I rolled over, shut my eyes and counted down the ticks from the clock.

I couldn't help myself, it was four in the morning and I was up reading my new books again. As soon as I get the boys off to school, I was going to get my required tool kit and gear for class, come home and be in those books again. I had so many new words to learn and new ways of doing things. The new challenge ran my anxiety way high. For once in a long time, I was truly happy for me, excited about my future.

"What are you doing up? Don't you have to work today?" Bishop snuck up on me chastising me as if he was my dad. "No, I'm off for a few days. I forgot that I traded with someone so that I could get ready for school," he looked surprised. "Why, whats up?" I gave. He took a few steps back toward the kitchen then came back yelling, "How are you? I mean, how are we supposed to make it with the bills this month?! You know I'm still looking and trying to spend the little bit I got wisely!" He exhaled as if he was irritated. My nerves jumped and my head spent around as if I was the possessed girl on The Exorcist. Who in hell did he think he was talking to me like that? "First of all, keep it down and I got my half of the bills. What are you yelling for?" I took over. For a minute, I thought I was Regina scolded by Spivey. I had to regain my scruples. "You know what? I should've stayed with my mother until I found employment because this isn't going to work. I don't like mooching off no woman. I..." "What the hell is wrong with you? We're fine for a while, I'm working and you got money saved up so what's the problem Bishop?" I closed my book and gathered my things putting them into my book bag. Damn! He broke my concentration with his attitude. I knew he was militant, but I'm sure they taught him how to survive. He took a deep breath and did what was best, walked away from me before I went completely off.

"Ma' can you come up to our school today and get me from class?" Tony asked with a puppy dog expression on his face. "Tony, what's wrong that you need me to come up to the school and get you?" I put my hand on my hip and leaned on one leg. "This boy is going to beat me up if I don't bring him my cars to have?" The hood in me came to the surface and before I knew it, I was giving him lessons on how to kick ass and answer questions later. There wasn't going to be any chickens in our house. "And Terry, you better help him if it gets too heavy for him. Y'all hear me?" I instructed. I was dead serious. My parents didn't teach me how to stand up for myself, but this was my household and I was going to run it like it was supposed to be. Stand up or get knocked down by me. The twins got on the bus with hope and courage and some socks full of rocks, just in case their courage ran out.

Bishop has been acting strange all week. He really hadn't said a word to me since the boys got suspended from school for beating up a bully. He said I was immature and incapable of handling the duties of a mother for encouraging his sons to fight. He's been threatening to leave me. I didn't want him to go and take the boys away from me; because we had gotten so close. I know I was out of line, but I was only trying to help them stand up for themselves. I should've been more adult about it, but I thought I was. Bishop and the boys were the best thing that's ever happened to me. I've changed a lot to live up to the standards that he set for himself and the boys. I stopped wearing tight clothing and I hardly wore pants. I didn't cuss nowhere near as much as I use to; I watched everything I said around them. I didn't even go out anymore. Mentally and effortlessly, I became a real mother; better than the one that ran out on them. I was like a domestic engineer without the ring or contract. All I did was go to work, come home and cater to Bishop and his boys! When school starts, then I'll be there, coming home and catering to them some more. I was standing by my man the best way I knew how, paying the majority of our bills until he could get on his feet. I mean, I gave up everything to be what Bishop and the twins deserved. Damn right, I didn't want them to leave. I invested a lot into the relationship because I believed in us. What would I have been without them? My life revolved around them. They were my family.

Dating My Dad

Bishop proved to me that Regina and Spivey were just donors who didn't give a damn about me. Anyway, I was willing to do whatever it took to get it through to him that we were meant to be, even if I had to put school off a semester or two to get my roots planted deep in the good soils of our family unit.

After receiving the phone call about Bishop being in an automobile accident, I panicked. I grabbed my chest and fell back into the wheelchair that I had waiting for Mr. Thompson to sit in. The paramedic informed me that they were in route to St. Mark's Hospital. It must have been serious and I had to get there, but my feet wouldn't move. "Do you need me to drive you there? I can take off with you," Ms. Cherry asked me. Ms. Cherry was one of the coolest Licensed Practical Nurses that I had ever worked with. She knew how much I cared for him from the stories I shared with her about the twins and us. "I'll be okay Ms. Cherry, just give me a few minutes to catch my breath and I'll get there," I whispered. Fear of his condition pushed me into first gear heading towards the basement to get my coat and leave. I cut my hazard lights on and drove 60mph on 30mph street zones. The highways were too crowded at that time of day. While I was driving, all I thought about was Bishop's life. What would happen to Tony and Terry if he should leave this earth? Seems no one was on the street, but me. I was in a zone trying to get to my man's side. I could feel his fear. *"Hold on Bae, I'm coming,"* I said to myself.

"I'm his fiancé!" I snapped at the police officer for asking me a million questions. "I need to see Bishop, please sir!" I yelled as I pushed pass him and some woman staring at me and went to the room number that the front desk clerk gave me. I pulled the curtain back. Oh my God,

Bishop's head was the size of a watermelon. Tubes were everywhere, in his nose, his mouth, in his arm and underneath his thin gown. I wanted to cry, but I felt the need to be strong for him. "Hey Bae, I'm here. Squeeze my hand if you hear me Bishop." He tightened his grip on my fingers. Cuts and scrapes covered his face. When he opened his eyes, I couldn't see anything but blood surrounding his pupils. I turned my head and swallowed the fear that was marching up my throat. My heart pumped harder and faster. Bishop held his head up and examined his body as far as he could see. He trembled. "Hi ma'am, I'm Doctor Chu. You're his fiancé?" "Yes sir." "Great, we're about to perform a knee surgery and we needed his closest kin here to sign papers. The surgery will be about two hours and he'll need to recover about an hour. Other than that, he'll be fine. Most of his bruises are flesh wounds. He's very lucky to be alive and only in need of knee surgery after smashing his head into the windshield." "Doctor Chu, thank you. What papers do you need me to sign?"

I kissed Bishop on the forehead as they transported him away for surgery. I filled out the paper work to the best of my knowledge and turned them in to his nurse. "Ma'am, I'm going to pick up my sons from school and I should be right back within the hour. Is it okay if I bring them back here with me?" "Sure. I will let you know how things are going when you get back." She answered. I smiled and left. I stopped for a complimentary cup of coffee and noticed the same officer guarding the unit and that same woman looking at me. Does she know me? Anyway, I fixed my coffee, walked out of the hospital to my ride and drove off to get the twins.

I couldn't explain things to the boys just yet. I didn't have the words. I told them that their father was in an accident and was in the hospital. "Is daddy going to be okay?" they asked simultaneously. "I was with your father before picking you guys up and he will be alright. I promise," I said as I gave them a warm, soothing smile. They kept on reading their books until we got to the parking lot of St. Mark's. We held each other's hands as we walked through the doors. I checked us in and we proceeded. I was nervous about them seeing Bishop all swollen and bruised, but the time we had left would help me to prepare them. "Tony and Terry," we heard someone call. We all turned to see who it was. The woman that was staring at me earlier ran over to hug the twins. I stepped back to let the hugs flow. I didn't know who she was. I know Bishop had a stepsister, but she didn't favor him at all. Who is this woman? "Hello." She said to me. "Hi. Are you kin to Bishop?" I asked. "No, I'm their mother, Toy," she grinned. My face dropped. Where did she come from and how did she know Bishop was in the hospital? Where has she been? I mean all kinds of questions danced around my head, as I looked her up and down trying to put the pieces to this puzzle together. I hoped she was concerned for the father of her kids and not there to take them from him because she thought he was going to die. Why was she there? If Bishop couldn't take care of them, it would be right up her alley to snatch them away, but she'd have to take them over my dead body.

Episode 9

Apple Dailey

Damn! Who could that be calling, letting the phone ring like that? I couldn't help but to answer it. I yanked the phone off the receiver almost hitting myself in the head. "Hello!" "Hey Shelby, it's me, Momma." "Oh hey Momma, I didn't mean to yell at you, I just got in the house with a gang of groceries in my arms and almost dropped them trying to get to the phone. What's going on with you? Is everything okay?" "Well, that's what I called to tell you. I- I- I- I…" "Hold on Momma, let me close the door, I'll be right back." *"I hope she spits it out,"* I said to myself. I put the phone down and closed the door, took off my shoes, got myself a drink of ice water, crossed my legs as I sat on the couch and then picked up the phone. "I'm back Momma. What's wrong? Are you crying?" I loved Regina and all, but, I know I gave her way more shoulders to cry on than she has ever offered to me. "Shelby I need to talk to you about something and it's very important. You might not understand, but I got to talk to you." "Sure Momma, go ahead, I'm listening." "No, this needs to be said heart to face." "Can't you tell me a little bit of what it's about?" "I'll tell you all of it when you get here." "Okay, I can be there in about an hour or two?" "Make sure Shelby." "Is Dad going to be sleep?" "I'm at your Auntie Pinkie's." "Momma, what are you…I'll be there as soon as possible." "Shelby? I love you." "Love you too Momma. Bye." I hung the phone up and pulled myself from the couch. I needed to get over to Auntie Pinkie's house and see what was going on. I bet Spivey done bopped her head again. I hope that this time she'll stay where she's at, in green pastures safe and sound.

    I cleaned the house and cooked dinner for Bishop and the boys, leaving them a posted note on the refrigerator with a smiley face. I wish I

Dating My Dad

could stay safely wrapped in the bliss of this relationship and never come out because life with them was a breeze; until I would have to leave them and go deep into the pile of mess I came from to save somebody. Like Regina, I tried to avoid contact at all times to regulate the waves of negativity. Still, all the years of Spivey and his ways and Regina and her mess, got to me as soon as I caught a whiff of it. Bishop and the twins were my safe-haven, a reward for the hell I've been through and I'd do just about anything to protect that.

    The cold air hit my warm body like I had been struck by lightning. I pulled my belt tighter on my jacket to block the cool crisp air and ran to my car. I patiently sat there warming the car up thinking of what was to come. I was glad not to be living with Spivey and all of the stress anymore. However, I didn't want that man putting his hands on Regina like she was some kind of stray animal that no one cared for either. Regina might have to come and live with me. I just never knew with them two. I'd discuss the arrangements with Bishop if necessary. I braked and put the car in "D" and smashed off. I'd better stop at the store to get some cigarettes; knowing it could be a long visit.

    If I had a gun, I wouldn't be standing here crying staring at Regina's bruised face; I'd be stationed at Spivey's bedside with the smell of gun smoke in my nostrils giving me the sensation of relief for taking us out of his misery forever. Instead, I was sitting there hoping Regina had enough because I had. "Shelby before you say anything, take a drink with your Aunt Pinkie?" Auntie Pinkie coached. She probably saw the blood pumping in my heart through my shirt. "That's okay Auntie Pinkie. If I drink something now, I'll be in jail tonight. Momma, what happened this time?" I placed my tongue across my mouth to block words from coming out that had dropped by from my brain and waited for Regina to answer. "Don't worry about me Shelby. I'm okay. Me and your dad had a few words and things got out of hand, but God took care of me and let me make it here to Pinkie's and I'll be here a minute or two to get my head right," she said as she took a sip from her cup and broke a phony smile. "You know what Momma, I'm not going to tell you what I really want to say, but I will say this, you're too old Momma, too old and worth much more than he will ever give you!" "Now I said I'm fine and leave it alone. I didn't ask you to come over here so you can scold me like you gave me life. I wanted you to come so that we can talk and pray about some things." She took another sip from her cup, then rose up to refill it with more hot water; then begin to tell me of what happened a few nights before between her and Spivey. Thank God Craig and George King where there or she'd be dead according to her side of the story.

"Forget that Momma! You didn't just call me over here to pray and talk when you knew that when I saw your face like this and hear that crap it would upset me enough to make me hurt that man." "Settle down whippa snappa," Auntie Pinkie added. "Yes, ma'am, I'm sorry, but I almost hate him. And Momma keeps going back and I got a life to live and it hurts and embarrasses me at the same time to be dealing with this." I thought Regina was going to chop my head clean off. She gave me a look that cut my words in two. "Stop sassing me, that two-faced creep you got ain't no different from your dad and you're going find that out. Girl open your eyes, don't you see the curse that's upon you? I want to pray because I didn't see it before, but I see it now." Fear pumped my heart.

Regina was serious and I felt it, she had my attention. "What curse Momma?" Regina bowed her head and we followed, she began praying, *"Father in Heaven what curse is it that is over me, what do she mean when she prayed to You about me understanding her mistake and stuff. Answer me Big God please? Oh, yeah, it's me, Shelby Spivey.* I didn't hear anything Regina prayed. I wanted to ask for myself what was going on. My mind felt like bumper cars, it kept bumping into the harsh thoughts. I rubbed Regina's face and combed her hair and put a high ponytail in it as I listen to them try to recap the sermon they went to that set them mentally free with the truthful knowledge of the curse many women had on them. Nonetheless, I didn't take it personal that their pastor meant us. Anyway, we laughed; chit chatted and laughed a bit more before I couldn't take it anymore. "Momma, what is it that you have to tell me?"" My eyes got bucked alarming her of my annoyance. Auntie Pinkie held Regina's hand gently and said, "Come clean Reggie it's time. I'm here for you and I'm not going anywhere. I promise." "Okay," Regina agreed and turned to me and without a pause; she let it out that I had a generational curse on me. She said their husbands or common law mates beat all the women on her side of the family. "Why do you think I'm single Shelby and won't let a man live with me?" Auntie Pinkie joined in. "I don't know, but since you asked, I thought you just didn't want any man to be controlling you. And you just wanted to be alone with your pets." I looked over at the bottle again to see if it could solve my problems if I took a swig.

I didn't know what to think after listening to the two women I loved the most tell me that I had a curse on me. Truth be told, I just wanted to get the hell out of there. They were spooking me out. Plus, the fact that there may be some truth to their warnings was starting to take over my attention. So what was I supposed to do about it? Was I supposed to just accept it then let every man I get with from here on destroy me? Alternatively, was I going to be alone for the rest of my life because of some curse? Auntie Pinkie and Regina have been into church and stuff lately so maybe they're just over thinking things. I don't know, but whatever they warned me of, did it have anything to do with what's been going on in my life with men. I have to get home to my safe-haven. "Momma I love you and I'ma see you later okay, I need to go home and get ready for school and work," I said as I hugged her and Auntie Pinkie. Then I stood up to put my coat and things on for the cold, but the tears that rolled down Regina's face stopped me. Sorrow gripped my body as I was thinking that I have been taking all of this hell from life, then to find out it was done on purpose or a part of God's plan. Regina's tears disappeared. All attention was on me. "What?" I asked when I really wanted to grab the fifth of Scotch that was staring at me from the back of the bar, crack it open and jump in headfirst just to numb those nerves that picked my brain raggedy. "Shelby, I know this all sounds crazy to you, but it's true," Regina told me. "Momma, this is all news to me, I didn't ask for none of it to happen to me and I really didn't care to hear it, but I didn't have a choice did I? Well, I do and I choose to go home." I began gathering my things but Auntie Pinkie stopped me. If she weren't my aunt, she would have a scratched up arm for grabbing me like that. "We're going to sit down and talk this through. We are family, adults and good women of God." She put her hand on her hip. I had to listen out of respect for them, but to be called a "Woman of God" to a God that would cause me all the pain I've been through just because He felt like it; I was angry. It was just before midnight when I checked the time. Regina and Auntie Pinkie expressed and explained everything that I needed to know about their struggles and the curse. I bargained with them that I would try to understand. Regina wasn't as bad as I thought. I guessed anybody could do better without all of that dead weight hanging onto him or her.

"Momma, I love you and I am so glad that you decided to stay here and get away from Dad." For the first time I saw a real smile on her face. "Baby, the choice is yours. You're grown and I've got to get myself together. I just don't want you to be lost and uncertain like I was. But, the good thang about it is, you can do something about it now before it's too late. I invite you to come to church with us, but again the choice is yours and I know you'll make the right decision," Regina gave. I really wanted a cigarette. I hugged Regina, then Auntie Pinkie walked me to the door and said, "Shelby, some things take a little longer to change. Your mother loves you, though she may not act like it all the time. But believe me, she feels bad about the things she allowed Spivey to do to you. She didn't know any better; she has to live with those mistakes and so does Spivey. I told you God don't let people hurt his children without getting angry, but I promise you, God is the wrong one to upset and to be upset with." She hugged me and watched until I got into my car. I sat there letting it warm up recalling the new things that bombarded my life. I don't know what I'm going to tell Bishop, but I sure don't want him to know. His family is drama-free and mine had enough drama to fill his family and some.

Episode 10

I have never been with anyone as selfish and numb to others feelings as Mr. Bishop Styles. This man had a car accident; I rushed to his side then left him for a few minutes to drive across town to pick up his boys from school so they could be with their father. Did I mention that I held my cool with his sons' mother for the sake of peace, when I really wanted to beat her unconscious? Point blank! I was thoughtful and alert. When it comes to him and the twins, I'm always there, all ears, heart and mind, trying to be a part of the solution and never the problem.

Anyhow, I finally took off my super-cape and turned to him for support, giving him the details of my most important discovery and he turns all nasty on me like a cold plate of collard greens. I will never do that again! Who does he think he is to have me break my code of ethics, sharing my deepest troubles with him expecting him to stretch himself for me as he expects of me? Bishop shrugged his shoulders more than he spoke not saying too much at all. "You don't have to be with anyone that you don't want to be with Shelby," he pursed his lips and shrugged his shoulders again as if I was taking the whole thing personal. It felt weird, him giving me the cold shoulder like that and for what?

"Bae, what do that have to do with anything I said to you? I was just asking you what you thought about my situation. And you gave me nothing," I jumped up to fix me some warm coffee. "I don't know what the hell to say. You will figure it out if you just sit still and watch. I got other things on my mind right now. I told you that I didn't want to talk about anything right now! Are you going to get my car fixed? Are you going to pay for what it's going cost to fix it? If you're not, you can shut up talking to me about everything else!" he slammed his plate of hot food to the floor and stormed out of the house. My heart was pumping 30mph. I couldn't believe he snapped. *"What in the hell is wrong with him? What did I say to cause him to go off on me for wanting help?"* I thought to myself.

Cleaning has always relaxed me so that's what I did. I cleaned the kitchen, the bathroom, the living and dining room and was on my way to the boys' room when I heard some whisperings. Terry came running up to me, "I love you Mommy-I mean Ms. Shelby." What did he say? Where did that come from? I hugged Terry back. "I love you too. Are you hungry?" "Yep, I mean yes," he gave me a big smile. I looked down into those beautiful eyes of his and reconsidered leaving Bishop. "Okay, now you can go get Tony and you both get washed up, your food will be ready when you're done." "Ms. Shelby? Me love you a lot, this whole much," he spread his arms open as far as he could. "Me love you too Terry," I returned with a smile.

The twins and I ate together while Bishop slumped down in his chair looking mischievous. If he was waiting for me to apologize to him, he had better think again. If it weren't for love, his side of the lease would be terminated. Truth be told, I was so sick and tired of Bishop's crabbiness. Lately, he's been snappy and I tried with the strength of an army to overlook all of his tantrums but today was the breaking point for me. It's not as if we've been together that long for him to think he could take it for granted. Something is bothering him so deep that it's wedging a crater between us. I really hope he grabs a hold of himself and duct tape his mouth shut so we can go back to the open field of love we toiled and weeded so hard to have. "Tony and Terry it's time for bed," Bishop demanded from the living room. He's just being mean. "Bae, they're not done eating," I gave back. The boys were obedient and rose from the table leaving their plates full of food. "They my boys and I'm their dad and I said it's time for them to go to bed!" "Ex-x-cuse you Bishop," I said sarcastically. *"He has lost his everlasting mind, talking to me like that and in front of the boys at that."* Terry and Tony broke out up the stairs in fear. I shook my head letting him know that he was out of line. He walked near me staring at me as if I said one more word there would be no telling what he would be forced to do. I wish he would.

The house seemed cold and empty though it was fully heated with four bodies in it. I ignored Bishop for the rest of my evening as I straightened up the mess and prepared for my long day of work and school trying to come up with a solution to an unknown problem. I wanted so bad to talk with him and ask what was bugging him to cause him to be so angry with me. I've always heard Auntie Pinkie say that a man in his rage was nothing for me to try to figure out; it was a blunt clue for me to get away which is why I disregarded Bishop's anger. Once I went through my checklist of, what did I do's, then I left it alone. He could be upset because he's not having any luck finding a job. Yet the fire in me wanted more fluid so that I could blaze and go off, but I'll just have to remain calm for the sake of the boys and peace. Speaking of them, I must be the only one that cares because I managed to prepare their lunches and iron their clothes for school while Mr. Bishop Styles gets to pull rank with them belonging to him.

I paced the floor with my hand on my hip like I was a prosecuting attorney with a whole lot of good convicting evidence getting ready to send Bishop to jail for the rest of his life. I scrambled around in my jacket pockets and my purse hoping to have one more cigarette left. I believe I smoked a whole pack on the way home to keep from running over somebody. I was frustrated because they weren't driving fast enough.

In the mist of searching for a cigarette to calm my nerves, I lost it. As soon as I got a tiny glimpse from my peripheral of him and the boys coming up the walkway, I met them at the door. "You lying son of a Bitch! Your car got tore up because you had just left from dropping Toy off to her house from the motel after screwing her brains out all day when you were supposed to be out looking for a job! You lying sack of..." He cut me off, "First of all who in the hell are you talking to like that? And second of all, watch your mouth in front of my boys. Terry and Tony go in the house and do your homework in your room. I'll be up in a few." "I love you Ms. Shelby," Terry gave. "Me too Ms. Shelby," Tony added. I smiled trying to return the love the best I could as they walked pass. *"They didn't ask to be born to a father and a mother that was as selfish,"* I thought to myself.

Bishop cuffed my arm and pulled me to the living room. "Bishop now is not the time for you to act stupid with me. Let me go now!" I snatched away from his grip. "Okay, but what are you talking about?" he asked me with a blank look on his face. "You know damn well what I'm talking about. You and Toy thinking of y'all selves and not me or the boys," I replied. I scrambled around in my purse some more and found one flimsy cigarette and my lighter. I lit up, took a drag and blew the rest in his face. "Bae, I went over her house to get presents she had for Terry and Tony. That's all. Where did you get all that other stuff from?" he began. "Bishop you didn't bring any presents to the house and there wasn't any in your car and you didn't tell me that she was back in the picture. Again, you said nothing. So why are you lying?" I took another long drag and blew the rest in his face. That nut sat there and let me do it. Normally, he'd be all over me about smoking period, let alone smoking in the house and blowing it in his face. Now that he was is in trouble, all of a sudden he's cool with it. "That's how I had the accident. I was so upset that she didn't have anything and called me over there for nothing that I lost focus and you know the rest," he explained. I took two more drags blowing the rest in his face before responding, "How did she call you? I know that tramp didn't call here did she?" I argued. "No Bae, she called my mother and my mother called me and gave me her number," he replied. *"I wanted to tell him to stop calling me Bae!"* "I told you your mother don't like me! But I don't give a fuck!" I spewed. "Shelby, why do you think my mother doesn't like you. Just because she gave me Toy's number doesn't mean she don't like you, she wants the boys to see their mother, that's all, trust me, she don't like Toy either. She was just concerned," he said. "Okay, but how come you didn't tell me Bishop? Don't you think that's something I should know?" I asked as I put my hands on my hips. I was steaming mad. Betrayal was an understatement for what I felt. "Bae I can't deny the twins the opportunity to see their mother, but I wanted to get the gifts first. I didn't tell you because I was too embarrassed of what happened because in my heart I knew I shouldn't have called her in the first place. Then to get over there and hear her sob stories about her disappearing act; I just hid the truth knowing that I wasn't going to let her see them again and that was that. Who told you about her anyway?" he asked. "She did. The tramp called my job, now you tell me how did she know where I worked?" I asked looking to him for the answers. "I don't know. But what did she say?" he asked. "She told me that she didn't want to, but she slept with you because it was the only way you'd let her see the boys," I said looking into his eyes for the truth. Bishop leaped from his chair yelling at the top of his lungs, "That Bitch is lying!" I jumped back and said, "Why are you so irate Bishop?" I thought to myself, *"She must have been lying calling my job telling me the icky details like I wanted to hear."* "She's only doing that shit to make you mad and get you out of the way because she wants me back. But I don't want her," he spewed. I began pacing the floor. "See I don't like it when people try to play mind games with me. I'ma hurt that tramp when I see her. Give me her number Bae, I'ma call her and let her know," I said turning defensive. Bishop stopped in his tracks and looked at me. "You got her number don't you?" I asked again. He scratched and rubbed his nose as if he had allergies. "What's the problem?" I asked. "Yeah, I got it. What do you want it for?" he questioned. "To call that tramp and let her know not to call my job no more or else."

He went to his chair to get his wallet that had fell out of his pocket down into the side. He pulled it out, opened a flap, unfolded another flap, and flipped up another flap, then shifted through some receipts, slips and credit cards, and on the back of a small torn off wrinkled corner of a business card was the number. *"Damn was he serious? I thought he went through a lot to get that number."* "Thank you," I said as he handed it to me. "Bae, go get me a pack of cigarettes please? I need more than one right now," I said. He scratched and rubbed his nose again. "Ah, are you done with the number?" he asked. I rolled my eyes unconsciously making a mental note of his new pattern of movement whenever he was nervous or maybe lying. He scratched his nose and bucked his beady eyes. "You just gave it to me. I'll jot it down and give it back to you," I told him. "When are you going to call her?" "I don't know, why?" I replied. "I was just asking. I'll be right back, I'ma jog over there now, okay," he said. *"Now his chubby behind wants to run."* "Okay," I said as I waited for him to leave me alone. He took off. My eyes followed him as far as I could see. I wrote the number down on two different sheets of paper, folded one of them up and hid it in my box of tampons, a place I was sure he wouldn't go. The other piece of paper, I laid it on the cocktail table in plain view.

Sometimes Bishop can be so phony with a dose of compulsive lying added. And thanks to him, I look at all male Capricorns the same way. He came in the door all out of breath like he had ran a marathon in the few minutes it took him to go to the store. Anyway, I needed to get rid of him so that I could place an important call to Toy and get her side of the story. My gut tells me that her side is much different than what he told me, just because he told it to me first didn't mean he's telling the truth and vice versa.

Bishop and I have been on a honeymoon for three days now. He's been kissing up to me. Whatever I wanted, he provided, both of his eyes were attentive to me. It reminded me of the first weeks of our love affair, but my instincts kept poking me in the back like a knife, warning me of his deceptions. I desperately wanted to speak with Toy, hopefully, she'll be open and honest with me. She had better be, if not, I'd beat her like she was a thief trying to rob me of my happiness.

"Bishop, I need you to call Toy and have a normal conversation with her and I'll be on the other phone listening. I need to know that I can trust you and her," I said hoping that he would agree. I was dead serious. I talked to Addison and my Auntie Pinkie and they both advised the same thing, put him in the hot seat and see if he sweats. So I went ahead with the plan and for that, Bishop snapped on me like I was a stranger asking for his organs right there on the spot with a chainsaw in my hand ready to remove them. Sure, I felt a bit pushy, but he wasn't fooling me with the honeymooning and all of that. Well, I was falling for his game until I spoke with my dynamic dual. "You know what? I'ma just take my boys and our shit and I'ma leave! I don't have to put up with this here. All I've ever tried to do was to help you out and be there when all else has failed you, but you got to go analyzing things, making them bigger than what they are, like you don't trust me," he said as he started pacing the floor searching for stuff that belonged to him and the boys. When he realized most of what he saw belonged to me, he cleared his throat and glared over at me. "What?" I asked. I put my hands on my hips and leaned hard to the right, letting him know I was on to him and rejecting his outburst. "What do you mean what? You want me to do this?" he asked with this blank look on his face. "Yes I do," I said and smiled. He took a double look into my eyes and said, "You want me to do this? Fine! With your shit starting ass! Hand me the phone!" I picked up the receiver and handed him the phone. "You need to do this. Dial the damn number!" I said as I tossed the rest of the phone to him. He hurried up and dialed the number before I could get to the other phone. By the time, I was on the other end he hung up the phone. I was still holding listening to it ring. Her answering machine came on. *"From the sound of things, she was probably having sex while creating her voice message."* I slammed the phone down mad because she didn't answer. Truth be told, I was jealous of her sexy sounding voice. I wanted to leave her an ugly message, but I needed some information and confirmation from her, so she was off the hook for a minute or two. I ran into the living room angry with Bishop because Toy didn't answer the phone. Well at least that's what he thought. "Do she work and what time do she get off?" I put my hand on my hips and leaned on my right side like I always did when I was irritated. "Hell, I don't know! I did what you wanted me to do and you steady picking at me," he said as he wiped the sweat beads from his forehead and rubbed his nose again like it was itching. "We'll call her back later," I demanded. "I did it already and I'm not going to do it anymore because of your insecurities. You either trust me or you don't." I wouldn't trust him cutting my toenails if he wanted all truth told. His eyes pierced mine for an answer. "I'll trust you after I hear you talk to her." I had my mind made up. He looked down at me huffing and puffing like he was a big bad angry yellow bear. Anyway, that was that. Rarely do I cook on Saturdays, but I walked away to the kitchen to prepare dinner for the boys and me. If he were to get hungry, he would have to fend for himself or eat cold bologna today, as far as I was concerned.

My day at work couldn't have taken longer. On top of those great eights, I had to go to school four more. I hadn't called Bishop all day. I was protesting and mentally strangling him for the interruption of my happiness. I felt like going home packing my things and vamping the entire scene leaving his dusty behind in the gutter with that mess. Bishop acts as if he don't give a damn about me, it's all about him and his boys. Well, if you ask me, he don't care no more about Tony and Terry than their mother did when she took off and left them. Anyway, I was disappointed in Bishop for the sake of peace.

I couldn't take it anymore, so I left school early, the words coming from the professor's mouth didn't connect to my mind at all, they slipped by sounding like blurs and riddles. When I got home I was surprised to find it empty; no Terry to greet me, no Tony to follow? It was 7:30 p.m. and very unusual that they weren't home. I checked the refrigerator for something to eat, grabbed me an apple, knife, and some peanut butter from the cabinet heading towards the bedroom to get comfortable when the phone rang. I put my snack down and hurried to answer. "Hello?" "He-ll-ow, may I speak to Shelby?" a soft-spoken woman asked. "I'm Shelby, who's this?" I replied with a big question mark in my head. I couldn't catch her voice. "How are you doing this evening Shelby?" "I'm good, who's this please?" I asked again. That was it for her questions, she had better answer mine or she was going to get my hang up special tonight for free. She cleared her throat and said, "Shelby first off, let me say thank you for all that you have done for my boys. I've heard many great things about you from them. And if you don't mind, I'd like to talk to you about them." My throat was so lumpy that a flat iron couldn't press it out. Vapors from my anger instantly kinked up my hair. I found myself scratching my scalp and rubbing my head a few to calm my nerves. Silence fell between our receivers like nightfall. "Shelby, are you there?" She broke in, "Yes, I'm here. You startled me. How did you get this number? Is this Toy, Terry and Tony's biological mother?" I asked. She caught me off guard. I was trying to direct my words to come out, but my anxiety pushed through. I put my hands on my hips and lean hard onto my right side. "Yes. Did I catch you at a bad time?" She slid in, "No you can talk to me." I went over to the front door making sure it was locked. Better yet, I went into top security mode and opened the front door and hooked the screen door, dead bolted and chained the inside one, checked my windows and secured the back door too. "Hold on a minute please?" I asked. I needed some water to douse and cool my fury. I took a good swig, swallowed, picked up the phone and spoke to her.

Toy ran down her credentials for the first 10 minutes. *"Nice."* I couldn't get mad at her for taking care of business, but I just wasn't sold on her alibi for leaving those precious babies with Bishop. I understand they're boys and she's the mother and may not possess all of the equipment for developing men, but she is and will always be their much needed nurturer. In my opinion, the twins needed her too. I just couldn't see myself putting some things as minor as a career or social freedom in front of my children, nor a family that loved me. I gained sympathy for her anyway, my heart wasn't cut out to be hateful for mistakes, big or small; she has to live with it. She was back out of nowhere to redeem herself and get what will always be hers, Terry and Tony and maybe Bishop Styles too. "Well Toy, I do understand where you're coming from, but I don't have any say so over what Bishop will allow or do with the twins. If he's got his mind made up, it's made up." I waited. "Yeah, but Shelby, there's something you don't know about Bishop and you're young and unaware of his past, but I know him like the back of my hand," she said. For a moment, I thought somebody else was on the phone, her voice changed. "Okay, what is it about Bishop that I should know Toy?" As I waited, my skin crawled. "Well, let me ask you something first," she started. "What is that?" I asked as I put my hands on my hips and leaned hard to the right searching for a cigarette. I had smoked about 3 from my pack listening to her earlier pacing the floors and didn't know where I placed them. "Has Bishop ever hit you?" she asked. "Hell naw! Did he ever hit you?" I questioned. I really needed to find a cigarette now. "Gur-l-l, Bishop use to beat me. We both met in the military and he was beating me at home and I had to call in a lot to cover up what he did to me," she shared with me. My heartbeat changed. I couldn't believe what she was telling me. I could see Bishop being aggressive at times, but a woman beater, not at all. "Are you talking about the same Bishop Styles or someone else?" I asked. "How do you think he got the boys from me?" she explained. "You said that you gave them to him. That's how?" I said, but I was being sarcastic. "Okay, Shellby, I cheated on Bishop because he was very dominant over me. I needed somebody to love me and for years, I thought Bishop did, but he didn't. He was more in love with us being a perfect appearing family than real genuine love from the inside out. I mean don't get me wrong, all things are good in the beginning, but once the honeymoon's over, all good things come to an end and ours ended in a battle. Because I had an affair, Bishop snatched my boys away from me and used them to abuse me and so I let go," she sobbed. *"I gotta quit smoking,"* I thought to myself for a minute then I grabbed another cigarette lit it and puffed away listening to her in denial. Then Toy took control of the conversation taking it to another level and blew my mind in the process. According to her, Bishop still carries a torch for her. He offered her the same proposition to gain visitation with the boys. "Well, this time I slept with him," she said. My heart sank. *"This fool is out here petitioning for her stuff, when he has mine here waiting for him to get it when he wants it."* I thought to myself. "Bishop and you had sex?" I asked. "Yes and I'm..." I cut her off. "You're a lying Bitch!" I snapped out. "Excuse you!" she replied. "When? Bishop is with me all the damn time, and when we're not together, I'm a work and school," I snapped and threw my credentials in her face, showing that I'm not as dumb as she thought I was. And even though I was young, I was a hard working woman and a student that handles her responsibilities. "Shelby let's not get carried away here. I don't have to lie to you. Bishop and I did sleep together," she vowed. Then I snapped, "Prove it to me than Toy with your lying ass!" I was pissed off. She was talking to me like she was telling the truth and I couldn't stand it. "For your information, do you remember the accident Bishop had a little while back?" "Yeah!" "He had just dropped me off from the Bora Bora Resorts. I was disgusted, sleeping with him after all these years. He felt like a worm inside me..." I interrupted, "Spare me the details Toy!" "Well, I'm not trying to be detailed, I'm proving a point to you. In fact, the twins and he just left me. We all had a meeting at the State Fair," she continued. Unlike me, she revealed all of that without a curse word or losing her temper like I had lost mine. My heart had grown cold in seconds. *"Where is Bishop?"* I asked myself. I wanted to hang up on Toy, but I had to show some type of class. I could at least have the decency to check this information with my man first before going off. I learned from Regina that women can be vindictive and sneaky, and the first chance they get to disrupt your happiness for something they want, they will. "Why are you telling me this?" I asked. "I felt like you should know. Shelby, look here, I want to be in my boys' lives. I want them back!" She went on. "Them who!" I asked. My heart skipped a few beats. "I don't want Bishop Styles in my life ever again," she released. "If that were true, why did you sleep with him then?" I inquired. Then I grabbed a cigarette to calm me, but it was no use. Once I took a puff and blew it out, I was still angry. If what she said was true, I might have to get rid of Bishop for trying to be slick. "Thank you for all the information and things, but I'ma get off this phone. You have a good night…" I said. "Shelby? Before you go, will you please help me get the twins? I'm willing to do whatever it takes," she jumped in. "Toy there's nothing that I can do about you getting custody of them. You know and I know how stubborn Bishop is." *"How dare her sleep with my man and ask for a favor?"* I needed to get off the phone with her a.s.a.p. before I lost my cool. The "B" word was breaking out of the cage of my heart and pulling on my tongue like a sling shot in full force ready to call her out. "Toy I will talk to you another time. Bishop and the boys just pulled up." I lied. "Okay, tell them that their mother loves them." "Okay I will do," I said as I slammed the phone down and puffed the rest of my cigarette to the butt. It burnt the corner of my lip. I put it out, turned the radio on, went and unhooked the screen doors, sat down in Bishop's chair and waited for them to arrive. Call me psycho, but I was pure mad. Ain't no telling what was going to come out of me whenever I locked eyes with Mr. Styles.

    I thought I would be more upset then I was after hearing Bishop's side to the puzzling news, but I wasn't. I felt a breeze of relief. He made it clear that it was a mistake and would never happen again. For once, I had the tables turned my way and it felt good to hear him beg and plead with me for forgiveness. I let it soak in a bit or at least until I tucked myself away in a corner of the house and shared the details with Addison over the phone. She snapped, "Okay, I know you ain't gonna fall for that bull are you Shelby? I mean what was he was going to do with you if they decided to get back with her. You gave up everything for him and those little ugly bigheaded boys of his and that's the thanks you get. You need to wake up! Snap out of it Shelby!" she coached. By the time I got off the phone with her my head was itching, I felt dumb, like I had been played for a fool. I didn't even have an answer for her because I didn't think to ask those questions for myself. She was right. I did give up everything, I damn near worshiped the ground Bishop and the twins walked on. In fact, I wouldn't have thought to cross him like that nor jeopardize what we had going as a family. I mean in my world, I had it all, and wasn't missing anything but a good man. And I just knew Bishop was him. I would give my left lung to Bishop if he needed one, just for helping me to see things I couldn't see without his keen sense of life. However, I can't believe he could just bleep me out of his life without a warning. He was supposed to be the older one that always made the better decisions.

    My stuff was gathered and ready to pack. I left the house to go to the hardware store for some extra-large garbage bags all to return and find my stuff gone. I gave Bishop a disappointing look. "Don't play games with me Bishop. Where's my stuff!" I put my hands on my hips and leaned hard to the right. "Shelby you're not going anywhere. I told you the damn truth and you just got to deal with it. How do you think I feel? I'm the one

Dating My Dad

that made the mistake of falling for her tricks. I didn't stay hard if you must know," he told me. I wanted to grab a pack of frozen meat and knock him unconscious. "Don't tell me shit else but where my stuff is Bishop!" Tony and Terry watched us from the stairs. I didn't care. Why should I? He didn't. If you ask me, they all were manipulators, like father, like sons. They didn't tell me that they were with their mother. No one dropped a dime to me and Terry tells me everything, so I assumed. Bishop's conniving behind probably threatened them into not telling me, Terry couldn't hold water but managed to hold that vital information from me. Anyway, I yanked his set of keys from him. "You know what, you're right, I'm not going any damn where! You get your kids things and get the hell out of my house. You don't pay rent on time no way, you ungrateful disrespectful punk!" I told him as I cased the house for my things and my cigarettes. "I'm not going anywhere either! And you better watch your mouth in front of my boys. You don't have to take it out on them they haven't done anything to your ass," he said as his nostrils flared, looking like the devil himself. I began laughing and kept on laughing until I wasn't angry anymore. When I started taking his house keys from his ring, he snatched them from me, "Bitch, was the first thing that came out of my mouth. "I got your Bitch, Shelby. You need to grow up. That's what you need to do. I need a real woman in my life not some little chick playing woman," he argued back at me. I ignored him and took a few steps toward the living room after spotting my things hidden behind his chair bunched up in the corner. I asked myself, *"Who's the damn childish one now, hiding people's stuff?"* Surprisingly, Tony came up behind me and grabbed my legs and said, "Take me with you Ms. Shelby, I want to go

Apple Dailey

with you." I tried to keep moving towards my things pulling him with me when Terry stopped me in my tracks. "I wanna go too Ms. Shelby. If you go, take us with you. We have fun with you." My anger with Bishop spread across my face like tissue catching the tears that fell after hearing the twins pleading with me not to go. *"And he says that I don't love the boys,"* I thought to myself. I took a long breath, cracked a smile then turned to Bishop. I looked back at the boys then back to Bishop and said, "You know what, you no good bastard. I will not walk out on these babies. I will stay long enough for you to explain to them what happened and why they can't come with me. But we are through! And I mean every word, you hear me?" I bent over to hug Terry and Tony, "I'm not going anywhere, I'll be here and we'll be together for a while. Don't worry. Now go upstairs, clean your room, and get ready to watch The Wiz with me. I'ma pop some popcorn and blend up some Kool-Aid for us." They mean mugged Bishop as they walked pass. I laughed. He didn't have as much power as he thought he did. My smile evaporated when he laughed too trying to get in good with me, it wasn't funny to me at all.

    Bishop followed up behind me for the rest of the evening apologizing for his wrongs, but when the boys were present he left us alone, hoping I'd change my mind and go running into his arms and into the bed for some fun. I let him know what the deal was. When I'm done, I'm done and there was nothing he could do about it. Besides, how could I ever trust him again, I reminisced.

    Wednesday couldn't have come fast enough for me. I was trying to behave towards Bishop, but I got bored and took off to shop. All I thought about in the mall was how good I was going to look in my new-sexy-hello-I'm single and free, come-and-get-it gear. I had about three more hours to kill before meeting Addison at Glaze for some cocktails and fun. And I wasn't going to that house until the last hour to get dress and hit it! I could taste the Long Island Ice Tea sliding down my throat, splashing into my belly and fuming up through my veins straight to my head bringing the purring feline in me out that's been hiding underneath Bishop's domesticated life of lies. I couldn't wait to get there, I was going to dance the night away and didn't plan on being back home until I got ready to or when the after-hours spots closed, whichever one came first.

Episode 11

What was I thinking, coming over to Spivey's house for the night? His place should've been the last place I went to. However, it was. I called myself being slick and sly by meeting Dennis, if that's his real name, over at Spivey's. And he didn't even show up. What in the hell was I thinking? Them Long Island Ice Teas didn't help much either. My head thumped a million bumps a minutes plus, I was cold. And me sleeping on a broke down piece of couch that Spivey probably drug in from the curb, wasn't going to make me feel any better.

Thank God, I knew all of his drinking buddies that squatted at his place while he was in Bluewaters Rehabilitation Center. Strange as it seems, though they were alcoholics, I wasn't afraid of them. They didn't cause me any harm. They were very good-hearted people who at some point in time had touched something that grabbed a hold of them and caused them to give up on life. They were controlled by a substance greater than their will to put it down. By the time they had realized, the distance between where they started and where they were, was too far to turn back. Most of them had been in and out of rehab and some never went, but I've been around most of them my entire life, like Craig. I've known him for at least 10 years. When he started coming around my family, he was just a young White boy trying to act grown, hanging out in the predominately Black neighborhoods, rebelling from his suburban life; Spivey used him up too. He always had a big bottle of something to drink when he came and when he went home on Sundays, he'd leave Spivey with some change to get whatever he wanted. In return Spivey protected him and welcomed Craig to whatever he had, making him part of our drug stone-cold drunk turned addict, still hanging family. Now he was in his late 20's and a around Spivey.

    I wasn't shocked to see Craig running things, trying to rig the electric meter to get the lights on and the heat working. Spivey gave up. His priorities became drinking, drinking and more drinking. And with all the weight he's lost, it was hard for me to believe he had eaten properly or at all, since Regina's departure. You'd think someone that was so depended on somebody else would've appreciated them more or at least enough not to let that significant other leave them helpless. Who was I thinking about? Surely not Mr. Shelby Spivey, he was too selfish and prideful to let anyone know he gave a damn about them. In his eyes, everyone owed him something and he deserved the best out of everyone that was in his company while he gave nothing; he was a taker for sure. He suffered lots of losses because of his insanity; Regina was his biggest one. Besides his mother (may she rest in peace), Regina was the only one who cared enough to stand by his side. Truth be told, I would love to be there for Spivey, but each time I attempted to get close, he'd shun me away, yet, I still cared. Well, nowadays only a few people stuck by him, but it benefited them as well. Craig and George King took care of his home while he got the much-needed help. Craig has been hustling to maintain the bills the best he could, cashing Spivey's disability checks and paying what he could on the rears. George King kept the house clean, stocked with food pantry handouts, and makes sure everybody that came by respects the house. Knowing Spivey like I do, he won't thank them for all that they were doing. Most likely, he'll find something wrong with everything and put them out as soon as he got there. All I knew is that he was blessed to have them. As for Regina and me, we were all he had and he ran us off.

Anyway, as I mentioned earlier, I felt safe being there although I was on some childish stuff. And though I couldn't stand Spivey, I had to admit that I still wanted to see him. *"I didn't understand it at all, how could I not like a person so much, but when they're down and out, I'd feel sorry for them. Even if I had every right not to feel a thing because of the way they mistreated me?"* That would be how I felt being there without seeing his mean face complaining about everything.

Thank God, Bishop didn't know where I was or he would've been there interrupting my peace and quiet. I hung out a few days at Spivey's house, sipping a little bit and receiving good advice from male points of views. They told me just about all they knew about the way men operate. George King told me to be free as long as I could. "You made it this far without getting pregnant, why stop now. Tell that fool to kiss your pretty toe and be on his way," the entire household laughed.

Craig pleaded with me to leave Bishop. His argument was that I was too young to be tied down with other people's problems and that I shouldn't be caught up into a family that I didn't create. It hurt, but I swallowed all their advice like it was a gallon of orange juice with pulp and I don't like pulp at all.

Sunday morning came and I was on my way to the kitchen to fix us all some breakfast when I noticed that Craig was the only one up. "I'm getting ready to fix something to eat; you hungry Craig?" He sat up wiping the cornbread crust from the corners of his eyes. "Sure, what are you cooking?" he smiled. "Whatever's in there?" I returned. Something in me told me to ask him a question that I been having dreams about, so I did. "Craig, do you know who God is?" I looked to him for the answer. "Sure. What do you want to know?" he said as his eyes bucked. "Well, who is He or is He a She? Kazeem told me his version and called God Allah, the Jehovah witnesses said something to me before and Momma and Auntie Pinkie say God is a He and His Son's name is Jesus. I just don't know so I asked God to show me who He or She was," my eyes bucked and the craving for a cigarette jumped on my back for a ride. "Hold on let me get the Book." He got up and headed for the stairs. I waited curiously for what he had to say. He came back with a red hardcover book that read Holy Bible on the front that he had gotten from the bathroom drawer. I remember that Bible, someone gave Spivey that Bible years ago and it said Gideon on the sleeve; he never read it. I remember it being used for tissue sometimes whenever we were too broke to buy a 50-cent roll of toilet paper. Anyway, Craig told me a story about hell. I got scared; I didn't want to burn forever and ever. I realized that I had much bitterness and somewhat hatred in my heart for Spivey, Kazeem and a few more were making the list. Though they hurt me, none of them to me was worth going to hell for. However, I would still go to hell if I didn't find a way to forgive them. And according to Craig, I had done all kind of sins against God. Then he opened the Bible and went to pages only he knew of, supporting what he said. He read a verse to me and asked if I believed that Jesus was the Savior of the world from our sins and that Jesus died on the cross and God raised Him from the dead to clean away our sins and keep us from burning in hell. "Yes, I believe that, but what about them hurting me first, like when I got raped? I didn't mean to sin against God. I wasn't trying to have sex before I got married either. And you know Dad was cruel to me and my mother," I hurried in. My heart was pumping causing tears to flood my eyes, but I was relieved because I always wanted to know who God was and get somethings off my chest. Moreover, I wondered what got into Regina, shaking her up to finally leave Spivey. Craig told me that God was big and immeasurable; it must be Him that helped Regina to see the light.

"Craig, how do you know all of this stuff about God?" I asked as I tilted my head to the right waiting to hear his response. He cleared his throat and sat up straight as if he expected questioning at some point. "Well, I grew up in a missionary church and learned about God in school." My head straightened up and then I asked, "Well, why did you give up and leave what was so good?" Silence fell between us. I could sense that he was very uncomfortable with my query. I made a quick decision to change the subject leaping up from the floor to get going on breakfast. "Shelby?" he called me. I stopped and turned back. "Jesus forgives all sins and He loves you when nobody else loves you even when you don't love yourself. Don't ever forget that?" My heart grew bigger for Jesus just thinking about Him loving me unconditionally. *"I haven't ever had that kind of love,"* I thought. "Thanks Craig," I sent back. That was the best breakfast I've ever made. It was as if we were partakers of the Last Breakfast. We all ate well and were happy until George King asked me if I was going over to Bluewaters to see Spivey. My food stopped moving around in my belly and balled up giving me a heavy cramp. "I guess I'll go see him on my way home," I lied. Shame fell on me for lying like that after hearing and receiving the good news about God and His love and mercy. I packed up my stuff and made a phone call to Regina and Auntie Pinkie informing them that my outstanding debts of hell were paid and that I was saved. They were so happy that I could barely get off the phone with them. "The Lord has answered my prayers," Regina cried out. I was sure that Auntie Pinkie prayed for me, but Regina, I didn't believe she had anyone else on her list but Spivey; the only person she really cared for.

The drive that normally took 30 minutes to Bluewaters Rehabilitation Center wasn't as long as the five-minute wait for me to see Spivey. I wasn't sure if the timing was right. I wasn't sure how he would respond with me seeing to him at his weakest moments. However, the nurses being so excited to see me they, put me at ease. No one had visited Spivey in all the twenty-seven days he's been there. From what one of the nurses told me, Regina and me was all Spivey talked about when he was conscious. She showed me some pictures of what Spivey overcame. They split his body down the middle and gutted him out, removing his organs, putting them on ice while they scraped his shell and repaired the damaged tissues that were supporting his organs. His liver was as big as an adult catfish from drinking a lake full of liquor over the years. His bladder and pancreas were eaten away at like piranhas had survived in that lake of liquor. "Why did you take pictures of that mess and show me all of that?" I asked the nurse. "We take pictures before and after for medical liability reasons, but I like to show them to the patients to encourage them to stay on the best track to a clean and sober ever after. Nevertheless, your father is one hell of a fighter and lucky to be alive. He'll be here awhile to heal from the inside out and go through our 12 Step alcohol treatment program. And then he'll be released and hopefully, he'll never return to us again for repeated measures," I wiped sweat from my brow. I talked with her a bit more and I excused myself to the bathroom to pray. *"God help Spivey, save him from his sick and crazy self, if You can?"* That was that. I washed my hands and prepared myself to see Spivey.

    I know he could hear me although he appeared lifeless so I was careful not to say anything to upset him. I didn't make eye contact with him for the same reasons. I never could please Spivey nor get him to smile at me and now wouldn't be a good time to try either. I reconsidered and decided to go down to the gift store and purchase a bear for him with some purple looking flower set-up. When I returned Spivey had been rotated and was facing the visitors. I wish I could have moved that big chair to the other side. I talked myself into staying a few more minutes that turned into two hours. I mustered up a short conversation with him as I gathered my things to leave. "Dad, I love you and will be here for you when you're ready, Craig and 'nem taking good care of the house and things for you, so you don't have to worry. Get better soon and come on home." *"That wasn't so bad,"* I told myself. I leaned over to kiss his forehead, but he moved and I took it as a sign not to. I gave him one more look from a distance before I left. I promised the nurses that I'd be back to check on him soon. "Can't make any promises when, but I'll be back soon. See y'all then," I said as I pushed the big button that automatically opened the door and left.

    I said that I would be back soon and I did. I was at Bluewater as if it was my second home. I felt the need to be there for Spivey. He had progressed to sitting up, talking without slurring and walking to the restroom next to his bed. I'd try to help him, but he was so grumpy that I decided not to. I could laugh in his face or boss his weak behind around, but what would I accomplish. For the first time in my life, I witnessed

Spivey's guilt from mistreating me all my life was eating away at his face like the parasites that ate away at the tissue around his bladder. He could barely look me in the eyes. *"Forgiveness really works!"* I felt like I was a giant standing next to him watching him squirm around me. For years, I had been hopeless and helpless to Spivey and now that the power is in my hands, all I wanted to do was be of assistance to him. Yes, I said it. I felt sorry for him and my hope was that he learned his lesson to treat people well, especially family because he'd never know when he might need them. I want the best for Spivey; he's the only dad I've known, however, I wouldn't wish his pain, internal or external on anybody, not even my nemesis.

It was sad to say, but I think he was hanging on to a string of life to get Regina back. All he talked about was how he missed his family, and what he was going to do when he got out; hoping Regina would take him back and they could start a new thing. I sympathized with him, but I kept it real with him, but easy. I was certain that I wasn't moving back home and I was convinced that Regina was sick, tired and done with him. However, I didn't want Spivey to give up on himself for he was doing so well.

I was with Spivey eight long weeks through the steps of his recovery until the 8th and 9th step. The steps where they have to make a list of the people they've harmed and then make amends with whomever possible. I was on Spivey's list six times and Regina was on there twice. I was angry, it was one thing to find out your perpetrator was well aware that they've hurt you, but for them to deliberately try to destroy you, was simply trifling. According to his notes, his mission was to obliterate Regina and me. I told Regina time and time again that this man hated me and I knew that he hated her too, but she stayed in denial. I had to get my thoughts together, they gripped my face and changed my expression. I could tell the moment was awkward for him too. I knew why Regina ran away from him. She had known all along what I just discovered, but unlike me, she stayed with him until she got sick and tired. For me, that was my stop for me to get off his bus. If I continued to ride, I'd find myself on a lay-over far away from my destination without fare to get back to me. Nope, I just couldn't do it. Not for a man who didn't spare me any mercy. I know I'm supposed to be forgiving and all but, I needed to get away from him and cut him off as soon as I could get my legs to move.

"Shelby, where are you going?" Spivey wondered as I stood up huffing and puffing. I wanted to scream at him and hurt him with the truth. I didn't want to play up to him anymore. For once, I wanted to crush him, wiping that ugly smirk off his face that played repeatedly in my mind whenever I felt happy and free. "To the restroom Dad," my courage lied to me; had me thinking I could defeat him this time around. However, I couldn't. Something different was going on with me. After answering him, I left the scene quickly to keep from letting him know that he was getting to me. He wasn't going to get the satisfaction to see me hurt by his carelessness. Truth be told, I didn't think he was trying to be vicious this time, he was just being honest. They say, truth hurts, which is why I stayed in the bathroom procrastinating. I was contemplating on whether or not I should leave or stay. If I left, I would leave angry, carrying it around with me for days like it was a big pimple taking its course to disappear. If I stayed, I would have to swallow the bitter pill he just gave me then pretend that I was okay, fighting the temptation to go off on him, embarrassing him and me in front of the class. *"Get it together Shelby. You've been through worse while living with him most of your life,"* I said aloud to myself.

I paced the floors a bit more and decided to hold my head up high and walk out of the doors to freedom. So what if I had to wallow in it a few days, I'd be away from him and eventually it'll be over.

Episode 12

At last, peace had its way in my home. My semester was up and summer was just around the corner. Immediately, I picked up more hours at work to replace my school time, being productive kept my mind busy and the extra money wasn't bad at all. Bishop didn't like the idea of me working so many hours, but somebody had to pay the bills. He complained about everything, but I didn't give a care, Bishop just liked having the last word. He liked having anything to say about something, made him feel like the man around the house. Not too long ago, his savings evaporated and all the weight was on me. *"If he wanted to be a real man, he would get a damn job anywhere doing something and shut the hell up,"* I thought to myself. I didn't mind taking care of the twins, but taking care of grown men; I learned would burn holes in my pockets fast. Those types of men love to make plans for your money and they loved telling you how it should be spent. And to top it all off, they whined worse than little boys when they wanted something from you, at least boys are expected to.

It was funny how Bishop couldn't budget his money, but he managed mine to suit his lifestyle. He constantly complained of not having anything to wear. "That's why I don't want to go places with you because I don't have anything to wear. I've had these same clothes for years, they're getting too small." He repeated as if I hadn't noticed his weight sliding up the scale on me while his mouth tore me down. I tuned him out. I did not care about him having clothes that didn't fit; that wasn't a problem of mine. It was his fault he never missed meals; he never missed my paychecks either. Most of his fussing of not having anything, always happened the day before I got paid. I guess I was supposed to stop and pick him up some clothes after I cashed my check. I would've helped him more, but he was very ungrateful and besides, four x and his 52 inch waistline costs too much, moreover, he had responsibilities and bad eating habits that were there way before he met me. Leave it to him; I'm supposed to drop everything to rush to his cry because that's what he was accustomed too. I didn't come into this relationship needing him to take care of me at all. And after the pain he caused me, I wish I would cash my check and spend a penny on his sorry behind.

He loved to throw it in my face of the counseling that he claims he did to me. If I would have known that him listening to the little bit he let me get in before he interrupted and gave his two cents would cost me, I would have stopped him. When it got down to it, none of his advice worked anyway, he turned out to be an impressive talker with no depth to him. All he stood strong for was the pile of feces he was sinking in. I couldn't stand it he thought he was slick. He irritated me, he reminded me of Spivey whining to Regina as if she was his mother instead of his wife. Spivey needed bus fare and cigarettes in between his SSI checks; he slowly eased back and spent up the money he had given Regina for bills and food for the month. He didn't blow his income all at once, at least Spivey gave his check to Regina on the first, even if he swindled back most of it throughout the month to take care of his binges.

Bishop was sneaking and stingy about his. I never knew how much he had or when he had it. And if he could get out of paying for something, he did. If I didn't ask, he didn't offer. He got on my nerves with that! Every month we went through the same routine of arguments. I had to snap demand his half or threaten him to hit the highway in order to get what he and rightfully owed! Of course, he labeled me as an unloving nag. Oh, well then a nag I was going to be. If he didn't like it, he could take the itsy bitsy stuff he came with and get out of my house!

Speaking of which, lately Bishop gave me a bad taste in my mouth every time I looked at him. I realized that I didn't like him and I knew for sure that I was with him only because of my attachment to his twins. Every now and then, I felt sorry for him too. But my sympathy didn't last long because all we did was argued; we didn't have sex at all, no kissing, nor hugging. After finding out about his affair with his ex, I shut the good stuff off from him. I just couldn't lay down with a man just to be having sex with him. It had to be some love involved, some hope for the future. More importantly, once a man stepped out on me, he could hang it up. Nevertheless, I couldn't leave him just yet. Therefore, he tortured himself lying next to me in bed knowing it would never be another hot wet touch of me ever again. According to Addison, I should've been gone because he was a lazy cock hound from the jump, looking for a mother to take over the responsibilities of raising his youngsters.

Addison and I had been running the streets as if I didn't have a home to be at with people in it waiting on me. She became my new partner in crime. Revengefully rebelling was an understatement. I just didn't care anymore how Bishop felt. I wanted to, but part of me couldn't care if our family was functioning or not. I mean every single time Toy dropped by to pick up the boys crushed my spirits. I couldn't handle it. To me it was unfair for her to walk in after all of the lost time and instantly take my family. Bishop didn't make it any better. In my eyes he didn't put in any work, he took me for granted and for love, I let him. He allowed anyone a turn at taking advantage of me too. I gave everything that I had, sweat, tears, and fears to stand strong against the powers that be of the strange relationship we had. Then just like that, without any consideration of me, he jugged me in the back with a jagged edged blade.

Each time I felt him near me, the security bars came up with chains wrapped around them and the censored lights flashed to protect my heart from him. And whenever he got within seconds of asking me anything, I snapped out as if he was attacking me. "What's wrong with you? I can't say anything to you. You don't cook, you don't clean up any more, you don't answer me when I call you. What's gotten into you? You and your little ugly girlfriend have been acting like tramps; bar-hopping probably hoe-hopping too. Have I said anything about that? Have I?" He said breaking the glacier between us, I promise you I saw him put his hands on his hips and lean hard to the right, mocking me. He was tripping. I wasn't paying him any attention because there could only be one queen in my house.

Lovely couldn't have popped up at a better time, with his clever behind. Addison and I were sitting pretty when he came in Club Cush looking all spiffy. He had on dark denim jeans suit with a light blue alligator skinned belt, light blue alligator skinned boots to match, and some dark blue tinted shades trimmed in gold. The scent of his cologne grabbed me and held on tight producing moister in my panties long after he hugged me. I had to admit, I was very attracted to Lovely, I liked his style. He was always clean from head to toe. What was most appealing about him was that he wasn't a show off. Lovely was very down to earth. He was a great listener. I felt that I could transfigure in front of him and not be intimidated, as if I was shooting the breeze with myself. His conversation was very intriguing also. I understood why flocks of women threw themselves at him, giving all that they had to be his main lady. Though he was retired from pimping, he loved to share his pimp tales with me. Which is why I didn't like to get drunk around him, I didn't know if he was trying to turn me out or just missing the good old days?

Lovely and I had this connection that made people jealous, especially Addison. Milwaukee was big, but the Black community was small; we all knew who the big-wigs were. All it took was one night out of shining somewhere in the summer time, and your business spread like chicken pox. Lovely had a repetition of pimping since the day he and his family migrated to Wisconsin from Gary, Indiana in the early 70's, but he had given it up after one of his girls was murdered on the tracks (street corners). Some pervert took her services, her money and her life and left bits and pieces of her all over Milwaukee. "That shit scared me Shelby Baby. Hookers still approach me wanting to be managed, but I don't even entertain the opportunities to be stressed. It's not for me no more," he said as he smiled and took a drink. "But if I was, you'd be a good one," he smiled again then cuffed me in his arms jiggling me to put me at ease.

Addison drew my attention and blood from my leg when she scratched me with her high heel. "I told you Bitch," she rudely whispered. I'm sure Addison meant well, but I didn't need her input or her bruises. I wasn't worried about Lovely doing anything to me and if I wasn't, why was she. Anyway, we laughed it off and continued on toasting. With him, I never had to pay for anything. It was V.I.P. whenever he saw me. You could see the envy on the faces of others, including his buddies. Addison took off a few hours before the club shut down. She made sure to warn me of how open I was being about what was supposed to be discreet. "You be careful and make sure you call me when you get home so I won't call your house," she said while rolling her eyes at Lovely who was teasing her. "Okay, I'll call you. See you later." I wasn't going to beg her to stay. She knew she was my alibi, so she could've waited for me, but I guess it was too much for her. Once again, at the end of the night, it was just Lovely and I hugging, smooching, and having the time of our lives.

Lovely and I grew closer and our alibis left us hanging. It had decreased to only him and me meeting each other out for cocktails and fun eliminating his homeboys and Addison too. As our relationship brewed and simmered, I opened up to him further. I told him about my background, the molestations and rapes from Kazeem, and the abuse from Spivey and Niko. I explained my fears and shed some tears in front of him. I told him all about Bishop and his affair with Toy. I shared secrets with Lovely that I couldn't share with Addison. Despite the fact that we both had significant others at home it didn't stop us one bit. We kept right on with our rendezvous'. I didn't know if sneaking around was the thrill or being involved with someone who was so real helped to spread my legs far apart in a hotel bed giving Lovely all that I had to offer. "Don't ever sleep with anyone without a condom, including me Shelby Baby. Don't trust anybody! You don't want to take nothing home to your people and I ain't taking nothing home to my people either." He advised me one night when we were at his playhouse. Lovely and two of his homeboys came together and split the rent on a decent place in the inner city to handle their scandals instead of taking the mean streets of Milwaukee way out to the suburbs where they all really resided. For it to be in the hood, it was nice, you'd think someone really lived there. It had everything I'd want in my house, even a blender. Anyhow, getting back to one of my nights there at the spot, I had too much to drink and we didn't have protection, but I still wanted to make love to him; it made me want him more that he turned me down. He ended up holding me until I fell asleep in his arms. And after about an hour, he woke me up to go home. As I mentioned he wasn't a cock hound, he was a special distinguished gentleman, not a little boy playing man thinking with his other head. He was my scape-goat, my coffee-break and my assurance of somebody else wanting me for me. I wasn't worthless as Bishop tried convincing me. I trusted Lovely with my life and he took good care of my heart and my body too.

Because of him, I ended up on my first flight to New York for a weekend getaway that turned out to be a shopping spree for the two of us and I didn't have a dime to my name. New York was the most exciting place I had ever been to. It was crowded with people everywhere, thousands of them all over the place. I've never seen anything like it. Entertainers lounged the streets doing all kinds of things, singing, dancing, and playing instruments, even magic tricks to get some dollars. One man dazzled the scenes with his sparkling sleeveless jacket with a bright white cotton diaper singing Elvis Presley songs. So many clothing stores greeted us as we strolled up and down 5th Avenue. Lovely took me to the original Gucci store and brought me my first handbag. I felt rich because everything cost more than my paycheck could afford and I was actually inside shopping. Money was no problem for him, he loved the finer things in life, and I enjoyed him sharing them with me.

We could've taken a cab, but we rode the subway over to the Ground

Bar. I had never been on a subway train before and it showed. Lovely chuckled at my energized attitude toward everything he was exposing me too. He enjoyed seeing me happy showing me things I've never seen before. If you didn't know him, you'd think he lived there the way he maneuvered place to place. The Ground Bar was stunning. I had never seen a soul food restaurant so sophisticated and elegant. The tables were set for a king and queen. The lighting was soft and sensual. The ambiance was sexy, with the live jazz and patrons. Soul food never tasted so good to me. "Oh my God, is that who I think it is?" I held my hand over my mouth trying not to seem star struck. "Who Shelby Baby?" Lovely asked turning in the direction that I was looking. I pointed right at Kid from Kid and Play. Lovely had this thing about him that gave him a way with people. He got up from the table as if he was Billie Dee Williams, strolled over to Kid, and came back to our table with him and next thing I knew Kid and I were taking a picture together. I couldn't believe it, but I was so happy that Kid was so nice in person. I use to think some superstars would be mean and nasty until I met him. After he took the picture with me, he and Lovely shook hands as Lovely thanked him and Kid left blending in with the party.

It was obvious that I was in love with Lovely and there wasn't anything I could do about it. He was blowing my 20-year-old mind away with everything he did. I found myself in wonderland wishing and hoping I could be his main-girl. My heart spoke to me saying that this was the kind of life I deserved. He was the kind of man I wanted to come home to me. ", *I felt stupid for being with Bishop. I'ma put his lazy behind out when I get home,*" I reckoned to myself.

We stayed one more night at the exclusive Exchange Lodge then it was back to LaGuardia for the short flight back to the same old sceneries of Milwaukee, Wisconsin. I was terrified of taking the flight coming, I had never been on a plane before, but Lovely ordered me a stiff drink to ease me. And we did the same thing on the departure home. "Did you enjoy yourself Shelby Baby?" Lovely asked, knowing good and well what my answer would be. "Oh, yeah, I had a great time. I couldn't live there, but I know I'll be back to shop and party and I hope it's with you soon." I smiled and slid my hand under our cover and gripped his private. "Hold on Shelby Baby. You awh right?" he smiled and planted a kiss on my forehead. "I'ma bring my people up here then I'll bring you back when I come back to handle some business," he said as he laid his head back onto the pillow. I removed my hand from him and caught an attitude. I didn't want to hear anything about his woman. As soon as I got home and got rid of my problem, he was going to get rid of his too and he was going to be all mine, and me all his. He glanced over at me and chuckled at my jealousy. Funny, but I wasn't playing at all; I had to have him no matter what it took.

Lovely dropped me off at Addison's house, helped me unload my luggage and gave me our ritual public eye kiss good-bye; where we both kissed our hands drum rolled them and laid them crossed on our chest, symbolizing friends for life. Thank God, Addison was there, I had called her from Lovely's car phone informing her of my arrival, but she grilled me to death for the details. "I'm on this man's car phone and you know it costs bank so I'll talk to you when I get there," I explained. Since she had become my partner in crime, I had to give her the dirty details to keep her with me. However, my satellite caught the envy that seeped through from her heart out of her lips into the airwaves of some of our conversations. Hopefully, the "I Love New York" tee-shirt will change the channel from her jealousy to her being happy for me network.

I stayed at her headquarters a few hours giving the particulars preparing her just in case Bishop's nosey self-asked her anything. She informed me that he had drove pass her house investigating, probably looking for my car. I was a few steps ahead of him and parked my ride in their garage and Lovely paid the fee they charged me. "I told you he was going to do that, didn't I? So now apologize for getting mad at me for not letting you drive my ride while I was gone." I said to her, "You were right, I was wrong. What else do you want me to say, Shelby? I didn't know he was so insecure, lazy bum." We laughed as we grabbed my luggage to take to my car so I could get home. I couldn't wait to get in my bed and dream about me some Lovely.

My goodness, I felt kind of bad, Terry and Tony drew pictures in crayon of me on a plane to the Big Apple, and they were so cute. Tony's had a dark blue bubbly plane flying over green grass and yellow trees with a footnote that read: "New York New York." Terry's had a square shaped plane flying over blue water into the clouds with a footnote that read: "I LOVE YOU MS. SHELBY ENJOY THE BIG APPLE, BUT COME BACK HOME." Bishop stuck them to the bathroom mirror making sure I saw them. Knowing him the way I do, he was at his tricks of placing guilt on me. I wish he would just tell them what's really going on and leave. I don't want him and I didn't sugar-coat it, I made it clear. That's one thing I learned having a dad like Spivey and that's to tell the truth, not telling it could get me hurt. I didn't feel bad about being with Lovely, technically, I wasn't with Bishop, so giving it up to Lovely wasn't cheating. We made an agreement that he would stay until he found a place. He asked if I could wait until he found a job, but I said no, if I would have agreed to that, he never would leave and I'd be miserable. I should've just told him to leave immediately as Addison and Auntie Pinkie suggested. "His momma don't like you anyway. Put that fool out and let him go home to her," Auntie Pinkie instructed.

Bishop tried his best to get my attention. He made homemade lasagna with homemade garlic bread sprinkled with parsley, just as I loved it and some brewed ice tea with the perfect amount of sugar to get my blood happy. Bishop went way out of his normal to make me comfortable. He wanted me off his trail and out of his tail. He hoped I'd forgive him and reconsider. He offered to wash my back and rub my aching feet. I turned him down, but he kept offering, shocked me; I wasn't use to him being so willing to pamper me. I laughed to myself because I didn't care what he did or what trouble he went through; it was over for us.

At first, I was mad about Toy dropping by unannounced to get the twins, lately it hadn't fazed me one bit. What I thought was so precious and sacred for me, had been tainted. I'm not selfish, but the memory of him having sex with her and him coming home making love to me, is just downright nasty. And I was tired of it controlling me, taking up my days and nights. So like a woman that didn't give a hell, I greeted her at the door with a smile. We eventually progressed to her coming inside, sitting on the sofa and having something to drink. Bishop didn't know what to do with the new me. He looked as if he saw a ghost the first time he came in and saw Toy sitting on the couch. *"Who cares?"* I thought to myself. The twins loved the new arrangements and that's what mattered most to me. On the other hand, I was making a bold statement to Bishop and Toy that they had no power. Funny, but when I started doing my thing and didn't care too much about theirs, then they seemed to act as if they didn't want each other anymore. Too bad, I hoped cupid would come and take the whole bag of his arrows and hit them in the behind, head, eyes, heart, and chest; whatever spots obtainable and rekindle the fire they once had that created the twins then they could leave my presence all together and become one big happy family. I hoped they would hurry up because Lovely and I were going to do us and we didn't need anybody in our way to be feeling guilty about. Bishop could keep staying with me if he wanted to, if he got hurt in the process, at least I told him up front.

"Shelby Baby don't leave him for me. I would never leave my people for you. I wouldn't want you to. If you did, you'd do the same thing to me. Ya unda- stan me?" Lovely schooled. I didn't want to hear that. I didn't grab strength from my heart to tell him that I was falling for him so he could crush my world with reality! Truth be told, he was right, it made all the sense in the world. If he left his woman for me, I would always wonder if he'd leave me for another too. However, I wasn't staying with Bishop. I simply wasn't happy I couldn't forget what went down, how conniving he had to be to carry out his plan right under my nose. Therefore, I wasn't going to stick around for it to happen again as if history wouldn't repeat itself. "Lovely, okay, you can stop with the life lessons. I'm not asking you to leave her. I was just letting you know where I was standing." I lied. My heart told me that he understood well how bad

I wanted him to myself. It wasn't just because of the way things were between us, it's just the way the chips fell. "What do you want to drink Shelby Baby?" I wished he'd stop calling me his Baby. It sound distorted coming out of his mouth after I poured out my heart. Calling me Shelby Baby use to sound like he had my back. "I don't want to drink. I'll just sit here and watch the game," I pouted. He put his arms around me and jiggled to relax me. Then he made me do our kissing ritual for public appearances. I participated, but my heart wasn't in it.

I had to vamp the scene early, I couldn't handle the truth and pretend as if all was well. As a result of that, I forgot about me not liking Bishop. I crawled into bed with him giving him the surprise of his life. He loved every one of my new tricks. I could tell by his squinted eyes and frowned up face and loud growling that I had perfected one of my new moves. I paused on the part that required a few more inches. He opened his eyes and we made eye contact. And like a kitten running into a mirror after its own reflection, it dawned on me that Bishop wasn't Lovely, I quit right in motion. "What's wrong?" Bishop asked as he gripped my hips holding me down so that I couldn't get up. I tried stroking him a few more times, but Lovely's gold trimmed bright teeth kept blinding my thoughts. *"Damn, Lovely wasn't my man, Bishop was. If I wanted him, I have to ride this out."* I tried and tried to continue, but it didn't work. Either the thrill was gone or Lovely had a hold on my body with a stamp that read: LOVELY'S PROPERTY. I pulled away from Bishop's grip and caught an attitude with myself.

I went into the bathroom and sat on the toilet hoping I could release what just went down between Bishop and me. I was more worried facing

Lovely than I was explaining to Bishop that it was a mistake I hoped he'd get over and really forget. Like the switch turning on the lights, I realized I didn't owe Lovely any explanation for sleeping with Bishop. "Shelby Baby I would never leave my people for you," played over and over in my mind as I sat on my porcelain throne. One thing I did discover was the truth, I was in love and it wasn't with Bishop. "Are you coming back to bed Ms. Shelb...I mean Shelby?" Bishop asked easing his wide behind into the bathroom door standing there looking dull and horny. "*Hell no*," is what I wanted to say. "Yes, but on the real Bishop I've been drinking and that wasn't supposed to happen." I wiped my head hiding my face with my hand hoping I wouldn't reveal my love for someone else. "Nothing happens that ain't supposed to Shelby, the things you did to me. The affection you showed to me was as real as it gets. I know I messed up Shelby, but you still love me, and you proved it tonight." I couldn't believe he was standing there speaking to me as if he was a psychic. Just like them, he couldn't have been further away from the truth. I took some deep breaths while staring down at my toes and thought to myself, "*Isn't it funny how people try to twist things around when they need you?*" "Bishop, if that were true than it was really meant for you and Toy to sleep together and be together now, right. As you pleaded, it was a mistake that will never happen again." I rolled my eyes hard. He exhaled, as if he was tired of me throwing his affair up in his face. He can get out of my face because his days of playing with my mind were over just like our relationship. "That good lovin' he just had from me wasn't meant for him," I thought to myself.

The shower felt good, but it didn't wash away my guilt for Lovely or the fact that he could be at home doing the same thing I just did, but willingly. I wished I had a way of contacting him to let him know how I felt about things. Bishop stood in the front bathroom mirror cleansing his body in the sink and trying to get me to open up about my feelings. "Is there something special you have planned for Friday? If not, I have arrangements for Toy to keep the boys for the weekend and I want to spend time with you. Whatever you want to do, I'll do. And if you want, we can go to church on Sunday." I looked over at him and rolled my eyes, he knew well and fine he didn't attend church. "No thanks, Addison and I are going out this weekend." I stepped out of the shower to finish drying myself off. I bent over to dry my toes and felt his soft chunky hands rub my back. "Stop please?" I wanted to smack him, but I wrapped my towel around me instead. It just didn't feel right, him touching me. He wasn't Lovely besides, he gave me bad chills.

"Morning boys," I stuck my head into their doorway, greeting Tony and Terry. They both responded and continued getting dressed. We've been missing each other in the mornings for weeks. Mainly because Bishop stepped up to the plate and became super-dad in a matter of days, getting up and preparing breakfast and lunches and getting them off to school. I gave that up a while ago I didn't want to continue misleading them like we were all going to be one big happy family; don't get me wrong, they will be missed, but the sooner things hit Reality Boulevard, the better. I believe they were expecting a change to come soon too. It was in the atmosphere and whether or not Bishop liked it, I was wearing it like I sport my tee-shirts, every day. Nevertheless, he kept on trying. He tried to take the pressures off me the best he knew how. Though it was too late, he tried to pamper me, but I didn't like him in my face or touching me plus, I could feel that he was out of his element. That would explain his stress. On top of all that, Bishop tried being sexy. After the boys left, I went to the bathroom to shower and get dressed. I could hear The Whitehead Brothers coming from the living room surround system. I snapped my fingers while sitting on the toilet reminiscing of when Bishop and I first got together, he was the one who always had new hot R&B music first. He'd bring it home and pop it in and have a little bubbly on the side, we'd learn the lyrics together and jam all night. That wasn't the case anymore, however, I recognized it as one good product of our environment that I was going to continue after he was gone, keeping up with the newest hits.

Anyway, I was singing in the shower when I felt his stomach nudge my back. Shock and anger raced through my veins. And my emotions had the nerve to try to make a run for it too. "What the hell are you doing?" I asked. "I needed to take a shower too," He answered. the smile left his face with the pride. For Bishop to be on the chubby side he was confident of his looks, what made him unattractive to me was his foolishness. Bishop lacked consideration for women, period. If he wasn't so lazy, he wouldn't have to manipulate females. I blamed it on his mother. "Fuck you Shelby! I'm going to get my things and leave! I'm trying everything to make your ass happy. You think I'm going to keep begging you. And I damn sure ain't gonna kiss your ass anymore, you ain't worth it!" he yelled as he jumped out of the shower losing his grip, his feet slipped when they smacked the floor. I tried containing my composure. I didn't want to laugh in his face, but he got what he deserved. "Whatever

Bishop," I concluded. If he weren't pacing the house still mumbling, he would have heard my response. I re-washed my backside, finished showering, lotioned up and got dressed.

"Shelby, why are you letting that man hang on like that, those kids ain't your responsibility? You too young to be tied down," Auntie Pinkie asked me when I called her home to speak to my mother. "I gave him his walking papers, but he won't vacate my premises. He asked for some time to get him a place so I agreed to a few more weeks, but he's got to go sooner," I explained. "He's just stalling hoping you'll come around. Mark my words my niece, you're going to regret not getting rid of him sooner. I know his kind, they sneaky and hateful. If he says something else slick, put his ass out. He got a momma to live with don't he?" she advised again. "Yes ma'am," was all I could say. I forgot to speak with Regina. Auntie Pinkie was well advanced on the subject of no nonsense tolerated. I wasn't brand new to her library of knowledge. I gained strength whenever I listened to her. She wasn't a dummy, she hasn't ever told me anything wrong and I respected her opinion.

I loved going into the little corner bars meeting Lovely, but my favorite one to hang loose in was Pat's. As soon as you walked in everyone had a drink in hand bopping their heads to the beat of the blues playing on the jukebox and grinning from ear to ear. If you arrived after 7 p.m. on any given day, you'd miss the fun. At Pat's, like most good taverns in Milwaukee, they did their thing early. You had a good time getting full of laughter, food and drinks and be home in the bed before the young'uns came out.

The smell of fried chicken and fish filled your nostrils welcoming you to a place some called their second home. The regulars happily received each other with a kiss on the cheek or a bear hug. If it was your first time, they'd speak to you, but after that, you were family and welcomed the same way. Of course, everybody knew Lovely. Whenever he made an entrance, it took him thirty minutes just to get to the bar. He visited Pat's every day for lunch and sometimes he'd go back for dinner, then off to the street to his hustles. He conducted business at Pat's as long as his connection's head was on straight. I had met him in there a few times so some of them called me by name and others called me Lovely. The bartender, Ms. Juicy Juice, loved to see me coming because I loved her cooking. Once she saw me enter the door she'd head toward the kitchen to prepare me something good to eat and if I wasn't hungry, I still had to eat. If I didn't, it would hurt her feelings and I couldn't do that to Ms. Juicy Juice. I enjoyed the atmosphere a lot; the drinks were strong, but cheap and free depending on who was bartending. Like I mentioned before, I never had to pay for anything as long as I was with Lovely, he had me spoiled. He handled me the way I always wanted. If only he was all mine.

Addison tagged along with me a few times to meet Lovely at a couple of his spots. She didn't dig Pat's that well. Maybe she didn't like the fact that everybody liked me? Addison could be so judgmental whenever we were some place and she wasn't the center of attention. She complained about everything, "I don't like being in these kind of places with all these old thugs and old hoes." She went on and on until I would excuse myself to take her home and get back to Lovely to enjoy myself.

One day after shopping with Addison, I purchased a pager and a new outfit from Daddy Longlegs' Beepers and Tapes. "Addie, come run over to this bar with me to see if Lovely is there so I can give him the number?" I waited for her answer. "Damn Shelby, I want to go home and try on my stuff. I won't stay too long. If you start acting like you don't want to go, I'ma take your car and leave your man-freak ass up there," she warned popping a hard piece of gum into her mouth. "Thank you," I added. We drove by The Dip on North 2nd Street, I didn't see his car. I made a u-turn heading south to Pat's, when we got a few blocks down I spotted his car at Tank's. I was scared to go in, it was too roguish so we stayed in the car hoping he'd come out soon. Lovely didn't go there much. "He should be out in a minute Addie. If he don't come out soon, we'll go in." "Let's go in, I've never been in there and there's a lot of cars out here. I want to see what's going on in there." Addison liked messy stuff and me knowing her the way I did, I knew she was hoping the worse would happen if we went in. "Okay, let's go." We got out and went in. It was smoky and dark. I couldn't see anything at first; and then this short dead looking man came from out of nowhere and asked who was we there to see. "Lovely, is he here?" I asked trying to pierce the smoke to spot him. "What's your name sweetie?" the dead looking man asked. "Shelby." "Wait right here Shelby and what's your sister's name?" "Addison." "Umm Addison's a cutie too, Ladies I'll be right back," he disappeared into the smoke. I pointed out the Ice Cream Parlor set up staged as a business. Lovely told me that some illegal joints did stuff like that to cover up what was really going on, big time gambling.

I heard a door shut, then out came Lovely smiling. I was glad he was okay with me popping up on him. "Hey Shelby Baby. You came looking for daddy huh?" he asked. Then he kissed me and waved at Addison. She waved back like she was swatting a fly. She didn't care for Lovely too much. "Look here Shelby Baby, you know what I'm doing, but I'm about to wrap it up. Here, take this and meet me at Pat's in ten minutes." He reached in his pocket, pulled out a wad of money, peeled out a fifty-dollar bill and handed it to me. "I don't need this I just wanted to give you my new pager number that's all." I smiled at him. He frowned as if something was wrong with him. "Okay, but take it and meet me over there in a minute. I got to talk to you about something important now. Order me a 10-piece wing dinner with the sticky sauce and fries, no ketchup. I'll see you in a few," he told me and walked back into the joint. All I heard was the door open and that was that. "Where are all the men driving them whips outside? Lovely needs to quit playing and introduce me to somebody real paid and handsome." Addison said loudly as we stepped back out of the way to be buzzed out.

I don't know what got into Lovely. He was so upset with me that he wouldn't let me get a word in. As soon as he came in, he reordered another drink, slammed it down his throat, wiped his mouth and grabbed me by the collar and pulled me into the corner. He went off about me having a pager. Where did I get it? Who bought it for me? How long did I have it? He ran on and on with his interrogations. "You fucking with my part-na June? You didn't think I'd find out about it did you?" Finally, he stopped asking me questions and I took it as my queue to answer. "Lovely what are you talking about?" I stared into his eyes looking for him to start laughing. I knew he was serious because I've never seen him act this way. "You don't ask the damn questions! I do!" Silence fell between us. Silence hit up Pat's like somebody had just robbed it. Everyone feasted their eyes on us. I raised my head up and pierced the familiars for some help. Lovely was overcome with something. I was spooked and about to wet my pants thinking he was having a flashback of his days of pimping. "What's going on over here? Lovely, what's wrong with you? You not gone put your hands on my sista and think I'ma sit there and not do anything." Addison defended. I was glad to see somebody do something. "You prolly set it up?" Lovely huffed at Addison. "Set what up?" Addison put her hand up in the air like she was swearing an oath. "She is fucking with one of my young bloods from around the way. He identified her to the tee. How she looks, how she walks, her haircut on down to the car she drives. And he told me about this beeper. I don't play no games like that. I'll hurt you Shelby Baby. I'm not to be played with. You hear me?" Addison raised her hand up like she was swearing an oath again, "Lovely, Shelby is my best friend. I know her like a book. She ain't no cheater and I ain't never heard her talk about nobody named…what's the boy's name?" I looked at them discussing me like I wasn't there. "June, Little June. Don't play Miss Addison; you know who the hell he is. You her best friend and she tells yo nosey ass it all!" "You know what you're crazy! That's what the hell is wrong with you. How the hell you going to get mad at her and she ain't your woman? It ain't like you don't know that she belongs to somebody else anyway, crazy ass!" My eyes bucked. Lovely's grip got tighter. He was angry because he knew Addison was right. I wasn't his woman, I'm not a cheater and I didn't have a clue to who he was talking about. Now I was mad, not at them, but the fact that I felt scared and stupid and in the middle of some bull crap in front of the entire crowd at Pat's. "Lovely, I just got my pager today. I got it so that you could contact me whenever you want and I would know you were thinking of me. I don't know any man or young man named June for real. He's lying whoever he is. You can take me to him and I'll prove it." Lovely turned me loose. I straightened out my clothes and stepped back slowly and turned away from him. I went to sit at the bar and ordered a drink. What a mess. "Ms. Juicy Juice, please make it strong." "Sure Lovely, anything." She poured me up a triple shot of vodka and mixed some Rosie's Lime in and slid it over to me. "Come here son?" she asked of Lovely. The music came back on as he came over and sat next to me. "I'ma start a tab." She told him. "Can I get a gin and tonic please?" Addison added. Lovely glanced pass me and mugged her. He poked me in my ribs so hard I bent over to the side nearly falling off of my stool. "Stop," I gave back. My emotions were overwhelmed. I downed half of my drink, but I was still shaking. "If I find out you and your girl lying to me I'ma put you down Shelby Baby," he warned. "You ain't gone do nothing to Shelby punk!" Addison jokingly retaliated. She started to explain reasons to Lovely reasons, but I stopped her. "Addison please shut up you're only making things worse. I got this! He's not going to take your word cause you're my best friend and he knows you'll defend me. I got it. And we will leave in a few. Let me finish my drink?" Something inside me warned me of Addison's motives. She knew better than to aggravate the situation. If Lovely jumped up and snapped out, what could she possibly do to stop him? I was going to get to the bottom of this without her help, and from then on, I will meet Lovely alone.

I was sitting in the living room watching a movie when I heard my pager go off. I rushed to my purse to check it. Bishop didn't know that I had it; it wasn't any of his business. I paid for it and I can give my number to anyone that I wanted to get in touch with me. I didn't want him messing with it either. I checked the number. It was Lovely. I needed to get out of the house to call him back. I searched for my flip-flops and keys. *"This my damn house, I pay the bills, don't I?"* I picked up the receiver and dialed his number. "Somebody page me?" I asked like I didn't recognize his number. I knew Lovely's numbers by heart. "I need to see you. Where you at?" he aggressively asked. "I'm at home. Where do you want me to meet you?" "Meet me at Pat's in about one hour. Don't be late Shelby Baby." "I'll be there." "Where that niggah at?" he chuckled. "He's here, but so what. You already know I don't care about him like that. I need to get ready I'll see you in a minute." "Awh right Shelby Baby." "Bye," I hung up the receiver and there he was. Bishop was standing there huffing and puffing like the big bad wolf as I turned around. My gut told me he had been posted there the entire time listening to my every word. "So you don't care anymore about me and my boys? We can get our shit and get out of your place now if that's the case." I rolled my eyes hard enough at him to knock him through the doorway onto the kitchen floor. My heart pumped with fear, but I didn't care. "Whatever Bishop, I'm about to leave and you can do the same. Ain't nothing holding you here." He took a few steps toward me. I flopped down on the love seat irritated at his point of view, "One day Shelby you're going to see and I won't be here to help you. What kind of man wants another man's woman? I had you all wrong. I thought you were smarter than that. He just wants to fuck you and that's it. Why do you think he's okay with you being with me?" I hated it when he tried to lecture me. I stood to my feet putting my hands on my hips and leaning hard to the right. "Look Bishop, I don't know what you are talking about. But he doesn't know about you and you don't know about him, so like I said, you can leave as well. You don't have to wait until next week," he put his head down and paced the floor. He lifted his head and I thought I was staring the devil in the face. "Bishop I got to go, you done?" I was rescued. He wasn't about to hit me. I picked up my keys from the couch and headed towards the bathroom to get ready to see my real man. "Go be with that man! I don't care! He ain't gonna do nothing, but dog your stupid ass out!" I slammed the door so hard the mirror and shower curtain shook. Bishop always tried to make me look like the bad guy. He's the one that started this mess, sleeping around on me with his ex. Tony and Terry hadn't been home much, but I have noticed that whenever they're around Bishop tries to pick a fight with me about my whereabouts.

Anyway Lovely appeared happy to see me. "Whatcha drinking Shelby Baby?" "I don't want anything just yet. I want to talk to you about something though." I swallowed the heavy lump in my throat. Even though he was smiling and talking kindly and plenty of people were around, I wasn't comfortable with him. "Shoot for it." He turned to me. "Lovely, I know you have somebody and I have somebody, but I'm in love with you and I would never do anything to mess up what we have. Man, do you know who you are to me? You're the stuff that makes my blood pump and the laughter that escapes me letting everyone in my path know that I'm happy. You are the first and the last of my sex partners; no one can please me and do to me what you have. I'm safe with you and you understand me. It's because of you that I went places I dreamed of going. Do you understand what I'm saying to you?" I held my head down hoping he understood me clear. "Gimme kisses Shelby Baby?" I stretched my neck out and puckered up for a sloppy smack on the lips. We kissed and I felt his happiness and mine too. "I talked to my people and he still thinks it's you though. Now I want to believe you, but I just don't know. You're young and fine as hell, so why wouldn't he go for you. He a good niggah too," Lovely kissed my forehead and took a swig. "Take me to him. I'll prove it to you. I'm sick of this. I'm no liar and I want you to know that!" "Slow your row Shelby Baby. You for real? You wanna go? Let's go then, with ya Bad Ass," he finished his drink. We rose up for the bar and took off towards the door. "I'll be back Curt, keep it running," out the door and inside his station wagon we went.

I was relieved to know that I had never been over on the block Lovely pulled up to off of sixth and Keefe. My sweat glands clogged up as we stopped in front of this huge powdered blue and white trimmed house. Lovely took a look over at me to see if I recognized where I was. I laughed on the inside at his jealousy and his nerve to investigate me. Like Addison said, I wasn't his girlfriend. Anyway, Lovely picked up his car phone and made a call, spoke a few words then hung up. Out came a slim dark skinned young man that I had never seen in my life. "I don't know you!" I snapped with the windows down and the car door open. I was on my way out of the car to charge him, but Lovely grabbed the back of my tee shirt and pulled me back inside. "Slow your row Shelby Baby, wait a minute. Close my damn door. And what you scared of?" he released me. "Lovely, I don't know that man. He ain't finna be lying on me like that! And you finna beat my ass for some bullshit!" I went off crying. Yes, I was terrified. I'd rather fight this man than to have Lovely to battle. "Shut

Dating My Dad

up!" he commanded with the collar of my tee-shirt crumbled all up into his big hand. His grip missed my neck by a pinch. "Big Dog, my people locked up. She's right, I don't know her," the man said as he stuck his tiny head into the car. "Good looking out man. I was going to have to put her down if she was out here like that. This here my Baby, my Shelby Baby, ain't you?" Lovely put a grin on his face. I rolled my eyes and wiped tears from my face. I didn't have anything to say to him. Truth be told, I was so relieved for the facts to come out so Lovely and me could get on with our lives and be happy again.

We hit Pat's, then over to the playhouse to make some passionate love. I cried and Lovely shed a tear. He didn't think I could tell he was mushy, but I did. I must've felt really good to him because he pass gas at the end of our session. It was unpleasant, but for him I would endure more.

"I don't wear no fucking purple striped panties Bishop, so who's the hell are these?" I snapped. *"This has got to be a dream,"* I thought to myself. I wouldn't have ever thought of Bishop to be so disrespectful and have someone in my house, in my bed. "All I asked you to do was respect my house and me as long as you were going to be here. Now you're trying to tell me what kind of panties I wear. Bishop, I have at least 60 pairs of panties and ain't none of them purple striped. I know because I didn't buy them. And neither did you." I snatched my sheets from my bed hauling them over to the light in the other room that was brighter so I could get a better look and I found a stain. "What the hell Bishop you think you doing?" He was standing there looking dumb-founded with his head down and bottom lip poked out. "Say something?" I dropped the sheets and turned to him. "What else do you want me to say? I told you I don't know where they came from. Maybe somebody left them over here?" I had to catch myself. I felt myself choking him until he turned blue and lifeless. "Fuck you Bishop. For real, fuck you. That's what I think about you and this mess. You'll get yours one day. And by the way, get your shit and your boys and get out of my house now!" There it was in my face, I was trying to be nice and fair to Bishop and he found the guts to insult me. I know he didn't care whether or not I was hurting, but acting like that got him nowhere with me.

"I told you to put that bum out Shelby. You trying to be all nice and stuff. Forget that. If I was you, he would've been out on the streets. Did you put him out?" Addison asked. She was the only person to answer my phone call. "I told him he gotta leave, but he's still here pretending to be packing stuff that I packed up weeks ago. He's leaving no doubt," I explained in my hurt. If I didn't know any better, something told me that she was relishing in my hurt. I kept on running my mouth with her anyway as I sat on the couch. I had the room dark with only the kitchen light over the sink on. I was waiting for Lovely to page me so I can get the hell out of the house for the night. I want to go over to the playhouse, stay all night, and go to work from there because if I'd stay home, it was going to get physical. I could sense by the way Bishop kept walking pass me that he was up to no earthly good. He wanted to say something to me, but he dared not. When they came home, he kept Terry and Tony away from the living room away from me. Tony yelled hello to me anyway while he got them some water from the refrigerator.

I called Lovely to find out what was taking him so long. I wanted to tell him what happened, get over to him and forget about this mess. He didn't answer his car phone. I left a long message, paged him and called his homeboy Don's phone, but no answer. Bishop kept peeping in on me. I know he was probably eavesdropping, but I didn't care one bit. Whatever I could have done to get him out of my house, I was willing to do. I dialed Lovely's phone again, hoping he was in his car, no answer. I got up and went into the bathroom to get some sheets out of the cabinet. I was getting sleepy, but I wasn't getting in that bed until I got a new mattress. I ran some water over my face. I needed to stay up to hear my pager or make another call to Lovely.

"Shelby, can I talk to you for a minute?" Bishop slurred out like it hurt him to ask my permission to speak to me. I sighed with irritation and raised my arms up over my head. "What is it Sir?" I asked being sarcastic. "Can I come in for a few minutes? I don't want to interrupt your sanctuary." I sighed again. "What do you want Bishop Styles, I'm trying to get some rest?" "My mother is going to come and help us move with her truck in the morning so it'll be one trip. Is that okay with you? We will leave tonight and spend the night with my mother if you just want us out of your face now?" He turned the lights on to see my face. I couldn't look him in the eye. I didn't want him to see how disgusted I was with him talking to me. My brain was burning and so were my eyes. "Bishop, I got to work tomorrow and I really wanted you out of here tonight so that I can get my keys and be done with it. You're acting like you got a lot of stuff to take with you. The twins and your stuff should fit in your car." "Well I'll call her now. Oh, can we use your car too that way we could leave tonight. I was going to send the boys to their mother's house." He's just picking with me I thought. The point of him telling me that the boys were going to their mother's house was clearly not my concern. "I'm not moving my car until I get ready to leave. What time is she supposed to come and help you move?" "Shelby, the boys finish school in two weeks can you please let us hang here at least until they get out? I promise I won't bother you. You won't have to do anything at all, I promise." "If you're so concerned about them finishing school and you know that you needed my help, why didn't you think about that when you decided to sneak some tramp up in my house?" He put his head down. A sign of guilt to me. Bishop stands strong on what he believes to be true. If he wasn't guilty, he wouldn't be letting me talk to him any kind of way like I have. "Sure Bishop you can, but I prefer you move when I'm here." "Thank you. Shelby, I love you I just want you to know that. The boys don't want to leave and neither do I, but I got to do what I got to do. But I want you to know that I'm not mad at you at all." He had some nerve. I rolled over on the couch giving him the hint to leave my space. He shut the lights off and walked out the room and up the stairs to check on the boys before going to bed.

Lovely looked surprised when I told him the news. He spewed out his drink on me. "I'm sorry Shelby Baby, it's just that it don't sound right. Trust me this fool lying and believe me if you say they ain't your panties, they ain't. He done put it to somebody you know." Now I was looking surprised. "Why do you say it's somebody I know?" I was thinking it was Toy, but I wondered who Lovely was talking about. "You don't get it do you Shelby Baby?" "Not really." I took a big gulp of my fruity tasting wine cooler, sat there waiting for him to school me. "Shelby Baby you said the underwear wasn't your color or your size. Who do you know might be able to fit them?" I was baffled. I couldn't think of anyone I knew that could fit those panties. I don't have any company over my house for it to be anybody I know. "Who do you think it is Lovely?" I asked. He blew air out of his mouth. "Have you considered your girl Addison?" "No! Why would you think it's her? She don't even like him. In fact, Addison hates his guts. She wouldn't do anything like that to me." Lovely reared back and held up his hands like he was under an arrest. "I told you not to put nothing pass anybody ever Shelby Baby." I took another swig and swished it around in my mouth to swallow. I couldn't wait to get home to ask Mr. Bishop Styles some questions. If out of his mouth slips anything near making what Lovely told me truth, he and his boys would have to leave my house that very second.

I enjoyed being at Pat's. I drank a couple of drinks and ate some southern fried chicken and French fries. I yawned and signaled to Lovely that I was sleepy, he was on the other side of the bar yapping, skinning and grinning with Don and Mike. He held up one finger making me wait. He had better come on or I was going to be sleep at the bar. I wanted to get in the bed and rest or let him caress my stressed body. He blabbed a bit more than came over to me hugging and squeezing on me. "Let's go Shelby Baby. I love you Gurl. You gone be my woman one day." He finished his drink. I needed another drink. I know I heard him say that he loved me. "Lovely you found room inside you heart to love me huh?" I asked sarcastically. "I didn't say that. You be hearing thangs Gurl." He kissed me and jokingly wiped his lips like my kisses were poisoned. "Yes you did say you loved me." "Did I say that?" "Yep and I wanna hear you say it again." "I ain't gotta say nothing you already know Shelby Baby." He put a big grin on his face. I wasn't laughing. I understood that I wasn't his woman already, but I didn't know that he could love me too. Lovely was always kind to me and I've never seen him with anybody he didn't like. He was not the one for keeping his enemies close. Maybe if he was all mine, I could believe that he loved me. I mean he made since about not leaving her for me, but in my eyes she shouldn't be there.

Since things had gone sour with Bishop and me, I've been with him a lot. Everybody thought we were a couple. They don't say hey Lovely and so and so, whatever her name was. They say, "what's happening Lovely and Shelby or hey Lovely and Lovely." We were together all the time and he still treated me like we just met. Nevertheless, I went along with the program anyway.

"You can stay here tonight Shelby Baby, but I've got to go home. I'll be back in the morning to get you okay," he informed me trying to brush me off. "You're not going anywhere, but out this car, on that porch and up those stairs with me and into that super-sized waterbed," I commanded. Who did he think he was taking me to his playhouse and trying to leave me there like I wanted to be there without him? I had a home to go too. Though I might not have wanted to sleep there, I had a bed to get in if I wanted to. "My people called up at the bar and said it was important that I came home. I'll be back. She wouldn't call up there playing games with me, she knows better." "Why didn't you tell me that earlier? You could have saved yourself a trip and left me at my ride." "Look here man. You said you needed to get some rest from your situation and now you tripping because I got to go. You'll be fine ain't nobody coming over here. I let the crew know that I was here with you and for them not to come unless the police was chasing 'em. Gone upstairs I'm coming with you for a minute to get you settled. I might come back if you act right." Laughter overtook him. It was contagious I started laughing like I knew what he was laughing at. "How am I going to get to my car in the morning for work Mr. Buck?" "Hey watch ya mouth now." Lovely hated whenever I called him by his last name. Only his mother could call him by his real name, Mr. Tracy Buck. People called him Lovely or he didn't answer. "I got you Ms. Spivey," he said as he mocked me. I laughed at him remembering my last name. We got out of the car and hauled my stuff inside. Lovely stayed while I showered and fell asleep then he took off locking me into the playhouse with no way out. The dead bolts had to have a key to get out and key to get in.

Bright and excessively early, Lovely woke me up with his gold trimmed tooth shining and bologna breath sailing in my face. "Get up Shelby Baby. I didn't know you snored. You look awh right when you wake up in the morning, not too bad, not too bad at all," I giggled at his goofy remarks. I had to kiss his lips, it felt good waking up to his face. I've been wondering what it would be like to wake up to him if we lived together, now I know. Lovely's private leg stood up as we kissed. He gave me something to think about at work later.

My day at work seemed short and swell; no one got on my nerves and I didn't fall behind with my patients. Nurse Kate and I got along just fine, my entire day at work was a breeze. I could use more days like that in my life. Lovely brought me lunch to my job in his brand new Yukon Truck. He caused a big scene playing his music as loud as he did. I wasn't mad at all; he gave the naysayers something more to talk about. Some days when I come in and saw my load, I'd have to fight to keep from turning around,

Apple Dailey

walking out and never coming back. I enjoyed my job when the load was evenly divided, but it wasn't what I wanted to do for the rest of my life and it showed. I couldn't wait until I finish my schooling. But until I did, I prayed for more days like that.

 I hopped in my Nova turned on my sounds and headed home prepared for Bishop to be loading the few major items into his mother's truck and his car. I dreamed of myself already there waving good-bye to him, the twins and hugging his mother then running back into the house stripping butt-naked, jumping up and down for joy. It was going to feel good to have my house all to myself. I'm going to throw a party and only invite Lovely and we are going to celebrate the peace. I can't wait. I can't wait.

 No truck, no sign of Bishop, he must've gone on and will be back with my key. I wasn't expecting to see that his things had not been removed from my house. He was supposed to take the major things now while he had use of his mother's truck and only have here what he and the boys would need to finish out school for the next week and a half. "Damn!" I let out into my empty house. He's got some explaining to do. I walked out to the porch to get the mail and noticed my neighbor Ms. Barbara Ann waving. "Hey lady," I greeted waving back. She continued waving, but she was waving back and forth symbolizing her needing me to come to her. I opened the screen door and put the mail on the window ledge then proceeded across my grass to her. "Yes ma'am?" "Shelby how you been? Have you been all right?" "I've been busy working more hours and things. But for the most part, I'm great. How about you; you doing awh right?" "Yeah I'm okay. Well me and Bo been wondering where you been, we hardly see your car home and we know you don't be having much

Dating My Dad

company at all. We thought somebody else done moved in your house or something. Until we kept seeing your friend girl come by, we didn't think you ever be home." My heart began pumping fast. "What friend girl Ms. Barbara Ann? Are you talking about Addison?" "Yeah, she comes by a lot. We know you don't play that and you have her to come by to check on your house while you ain't here." "She does a great job, she be over here like she lives here," my temper was boiling like a bubbling pot of oatmeal. A flashback of my conversation with Lovely replayed over and over, I could hardly hear what Ms. Barbara Ann was saying. *"That bald-faced lying Bitch,"* I thought to myself. I couldn't take it anymore. I was trying to keep my composure because Ms. Barbara Ann and her husband was an older couple that's been on the block longer than me and they watched and knew everything. "Excuse me Ms. Barbara Ann, but I don't know what's going on when I'm at work. Do there be a lot of people in and out of my house?" I tried not to look too surprised when she answered. "Yeah. I see them in the mornings and Bo sees them in the afternoon when he wakes up from his nap." Bitterness was taking root inside me. "Do they stay long? Women and men?" I put my hands on my hip and leaned hard to the right. "No woman came by except your friend girl. Oh, there's another young woman that comes by, but she comes to the door and get the twins and leave. Is that they mother Shelby?" I gave Ms. Barbara Ann her fill of dirt from me for being my snitch. "Yes. Ms. Barbara Ann, I got to get going. I just got home to eat I'm starving. You won't have to worry about the company anymore. I promise you this. I'll see you later." I assured her that she wouldn't hear a peep from my way after today and I meant every word. I made it across the grass, over a small puddle, and home without screaming. Thank God that door was strong enough to hold me up. My legs went numb right after my secured feelings left for Addison and Bishop. They were going to hear from me today and it wasn't going to be anything good. My Auntie Pinkie gave me a receipt for fools like them; gut them and cut them loose.

I tried to slap the stupid look off Bishop's face for the answer he gave me for Addison being in my house without my permission. According to him, Addison approached him with a proposition to help her sell marijuana. Addison wanted to be me so bad that she had to go the illegal route to gain what I worked hard every day for. "She told me all about you going out of town with your pimp friend and you're supposed to be at work, but you've been stripping down at The Gallery for months and she told me you been cheating on me with him and some other dude," he altered. "I don't strip my clothes off for a living, I go to work every day cleaning behinds and picking up vomit. If I were going to strip for a living, I'd be in Las Vegas somewhere not stuck here in Milwaukee with your no good ass. Punk! How could I be cheating on you when I'm not your girl nor am I sleeping with you stupid! If you wanted to sleep with my friend, you should've asked me. I would've agreed to it. I don't want you so somebody's got to sleep with you, why not her or Toy since they find you irresistible! Fool ass." I let him have it. I wanted to slap him, but he took off out the door.

I ran to the phone to dial up Addison. What she pick up for? "You two faced cunt! It's Bishop you want Bitch. Then Bishop you get! You betta not call me for shit Addison, shit! Do you understand? Lovely warned me about your trifling ass a long time ago! If I see you on the streets I'ma put you down. I don't care where we at. Far as I'm concerned you a dead Bitch!" "Shelby…" I cut her off with the click hanging up on her scandalous behind. Addison knew better, so I thought. How she could betray me for Bishop was anybody's guess. Was her envy eating her up that bad? She thought she was doing something slick. All she did was helped me to get to where I wanted to be much faster than my patience took anyway; away from Bishop.

I've been waiting for Lovely to call me back. I called his car phone 2 hours ago and left him a message. I know he's not sitting anywhere that long without me with him. He must be gambling or something? I can't wait to tell him about what went on earlier, how he had pegged them two correctly. I cleaned up my place from the mess I made in my madness. I knocked stuff over, pushed statues and crystal off my cocktail table and when one of my favorite pieces broke, the two love doves, I realized it was my cold hard cash that paid for stuff I wrecked. My anger didn't last that long. I cleaned up my mess and sat down waiting for Lovely to call back as I warmed up my glue gun to put my things back together.

It was midnight before Lovely called. "Whats up maine?" "What do you mean whats up man?" His tone was harsh with me like he was frustrated, but he needed to be corrected regardless. Auntie Pinkie always told me to nip sadness in the bud right away; "men got to be shown a lot of what you'll find out that they actually already know, but don't want you to know they know," I could hear him breathing hard like he had been running or moving too fast. I was trying to listen to his background when he interrupted me, "Shelby maine whats up? I'm gambling, I came outside a few to check my messages and I'm returning your call that's all, whats up?" "Well, I put that niggah out for good and I wanted you come over or come and pick me up when you get done," I inquired. "I ain't coming over there. That man might be in the damn bushes waiting to kill you. Look here maine, I'ma call you back when I get done. Awh right?" "I wasn't done telling you about the episode and what happened though…" He cut me off, "Let me know when I see you later. I'll call you awh right. Don't be calling my phone like that either it cost money to listen to them messages, hear me." "I heard you loud and clear boss." I hung up in his face. I don't know what's gotten into him, but I don't like it one bit. I thought he'd jump at the opportunity to hear what I had to say about my best friend Addison. He better hope gambling is the truth or he could hang it up. From that point on if people don't add up to something positive in my life, it is going to be me, myself, and I.

Episode 13

Spring of 1991

"Momma I don't want to hear nothing about how tight me and Addison were and how many times you warned me about her and her mother. Last I heard she packed up and moved in with her aunt and uncle back in Chicago. Please don't spoil my day talking about her at all right now! I'm waiting for this man to come back and let me know if I'm approved for this loan or not." I didn't mean to yell at Regina, but I covered everything I anticipated her throwing at me. I thumped my ashes in the nasty little canister they had outside next to the phone booth of the corporate building for the visitors and employees to put their cigarette butts in. "What loan?" she asked as she waited for my answer while I plopped my half-smoked butt in the can. "Momma, I'm going for a first time home buyer loan," I let out of my bag of secrets. "First time home buyer, Shelby why are you finna buy a house?" she asked. She wasn't excited like I thought she would be. She seemed more concerned about what-ifs. "Momma I got to go. I should be getting back in there and I don't have another 25 cents to put in this pay phone. I'll call you when I get home." "Okay call me back when you get home." "Bye-bye," I rushed her off the phone. One thing I didn't like was somebody telling me what to do with my hard earned money when they haven't donated or marched any dimes my way to pay any one of my bills. I loved Regina and respect her, but she waited too late to be trying to assist me in life lessons, I got the hang of it now. I'm like a bowed arrow held back too long and let loose straight ahead towards the target of life.

"Ms. Spivey, you can go look for you a new home," the loan officer happily informed me. "Are you for real sir?" I was so excited that a chill came over my body and my teeth chattered. "How much did I get approved for sir if you don't mind me asking?" "What do you mean if I don't mind? It's your money and your good credit that got you approved for seventy-five thousand dollars, not mine. You have a right to know whatever you want to know about Ms. Spivey." He put a big grin on his face. My eyes bucked and my teeth chattered some more. I was speechless; seventy-five thousand will get me a nice house in a wonderful neighborhood. "Thank you Mr. Dalski, thank you. What do I do now?" "We got some more paperwork for you to sign, but you can take this approval letter with you on your house hunting and come back when you find something beautiful as you are and we'll get on it assisting you with everything else," I shook his hand as he handed over the slip and I stood by the door gazing at the letter as I walked out. I ran into the women's bathroom to catch myself. I could barely hold my excitement. I glanced in the mirror and I exploded, tears flooded my eye wells and fell over down my cheeks and onto the floor. I had to see what it felt like to be happy, as happy as I had ever been. I couldn't believe I was twenty-years-old and about to own a home. Regina and Spivey never owned anything, not even their own words. When I get out of here, I'm going to celebrate. I hoped Lovely is ready to party with me. I'm in the mood for some steak and a bottle of Moet Champagne. I had a few dollars besides my down payment to splurge on. I was going to party hardy.

Regina left seven messages for me to call her. And I could tell by my other messages that she told Auntie Pinkie too. I wish she would let me make the announcements of my business. She didn't have the whole story and there she went blabbing off. I erased the last message that Bishop left, sobbing and whizzing on the line and saying how sorry he was and asking of my forgiveness. I don't have anything to say to him after all of the lies I heard he told my neighbors about me. He made me out to be some kind of cruel person and him a saint. I tell you, people love to be the first to fabricate the story, but they forget to add in the roles they played. Anyway, I didn't care, Bishop told his story and now he's history. He's going to be very disappointed to find out I've moved whenever he comes looking for me and I hope he finds out that I purchased a new home. In fact, I just might give his mother a call and inform her of my accomplishment so she can rub the news into her low life, good for nothing son's face. She's the type who loved to brag and boast, she didn't care who it was about, just as long as she knew of them.

I picked up the receiver and called Lovely's car phone, no answer. I left him a brief message of importance. If he doesn't call me by the time I get dressed, I'm going out on the town to celebrate alone, which wasn't such a bad idea considering I was the one who had something to be pleased about. I wanted Lovely to be there because he's always included me in on his parties. He wouldn't toast to anything unless I was there to raise my glass and I wanted to return the same admiration.

As I got dressed I sung like I was having my own concert and my diverse fingernail polishes on the counter where my audience. I was overjoyed at my comings and goings. "I want to thank you Heavenly Father...for shining your light on me..." I loved that single by Alicia Meyers. I was very young when she came to Garfield Park for a free peace concert, but I remembered the lyrics to sing years later.

My hair was perfect, nails glossy, my lips were glistening, dressed to kill and ready to get going. Lovely hadn't called so I took off. I ran by

Buddy's carwash to clean my ride and stall a few. I wanted him to admire me and give Lovely a call boasting of my looks. I stood near the curb causing car horns to honk at me and the boys and men inside to whistle. A few of them stopped and jumped out to speak to me. I blushed as they came up with some lavish lines. I really didn't care I wanted Lovely's stool pigeon to get an ear full then run and report it. After all, I did call Lovely first, we hadn't talked in days, so what was I supposed to do. I tried to go on with my life and not be under him as much. But I couldn't help it if I was hot and other men noticed me?

My car smelled new and was looking good as I pulled it out of the parking structure. I checked my rear view to see what the guys were doing when I left, just as I thought, Lovely's informer made a mad dash to go tell it and I bet that was Lovely on the other end listening.

I put my ride on the expressway headed downtown to the excitement. The thought of riding pass Pat's crossed my brain, but that was it, a thought. I smashed the gas kicking my speed up to 65mph from 45mph. The night wasn't about to get away from me, I worked too hard to get there. Top of the Hyatt, here I come. I held the tears back to protect my makeup; I was overwhelmed with joy. From here on out, it's all about me and what I wanted, life felt unlimited, not the glass ceiling that I thought was waiting for me, still I wished Lovely was there with me.

"Auntie Pinkie, I'm at the Hyatt celebrating, I'm not going to work in the morning so I'll call you when I make it home. I promise!" I yelled over the music to Auntie Pinkie on the pay phone. I hung the phone up and walked over to the bathroom. There was a long line to get into the women's bathroom so I grabbed my butt and private like it was an emergency and zipped into the men's restroom. They all had surprised looks on their faces, but I didn't care, I had to go. "Shut up, I got to pee, I'll be right out," I warned. I went into the stall, closed the door, used the toilet, wiped and flushed. I pulled my dress down, washed my hand and walked out the door. I wasn't the only one tickled at my adventure. Women got out of line and headed in that direction to do the same thing.

My head was banging plus I had the worse diarrhea ever. I ordered and drank my entire bottle of Moet Champagne along with everything else the nice White people sent me celebrating with me. I told them some of my hardships and things and they shared stories with me. They were more excited for me than I was for my overcoming and continuing on. "The best revenge is massive success!" Is all they kept repeating each time we made eye contact. We chanted those same words as we danced through the sloppy drunk soul train line. It was like I was on a whole new level connecting with positive fun people. And from the appearance of things, they had plenty of money and weren't worried about mine. They were shooting at me different avenues to help me get more money and keep it. "Real estate is the way to go Shelby." Little did they know, I was soaking it all in. "You got a bright future ahead of you kid. Keep it up and don't get pregnant and throw your life away on some punk." One lady's husband gave after he slammed a few good ones down.

I searched my purse for a cigarette and found napkins with full names, addresses and phone numbers written on them. I remembered some of the names and faces and invites that a couple of them gave me. I was invited to a yacht party. I would have to call them when I sobered up. But for now, I needed to rest with a roll of paper towel, 7UP and a bucket next to me. The last thing I needed was Regina pounding me for answers. I let the answering machine catch the last couple of calls, figuring it was her. I wanted Lovely to call and check on me. I hadn't heard from him at all. He didn't return any of my calls. He must really be busy? I hoped nothing crazy happened to him. The least he could have done was call me and let me know that he was okay. For all I know, he could be in jail or in the hospital or something worse, dead.

I slept a few more hours to rejuvenate my body. I got up and poked around a bit fixed me some fried chicken wings and fries. I made it through three whole wings before my stomach cramped and I put them down. I drank the rest of my soda to wash it down. I was dehydrated and in need of something sweet at the same time. Thank the Lord my place was clean and cool, I had nothing to do but get well. I will never mix drinks again in my life so help me God.

No one was outside except a man collecting aluminum and what knots on the streets. I could tell the street sweeper had been through the block because the curbs looked clean and wet, but the middle of the streets were dry. It felt stuffy inside so I opened the front door to smell the fresh air and let some in. It was a beautiful day, nice, sunny and warm. "It's a good day to go house hunting," I said out loud to myself. I figured people would be out and I would be able to get a look at the neighborhood of my choice and the people that lived in them. I went inside and closed the door behind me. I needed to shower and get dressed. Before I went into the bathroom, I slid over to the phone and called Lovely's car phone. "Yeah," he answered. "Hey Honey, what are you doing?" I asked all excited. "Nothin. Ridin around. What's going on with you man?" "Umm, I'm getting ready to go house hunting and wanted to know if you wanted to come with," I waited. "I'm with my people right now let me call you back when I get to where we headed you know this phone cost money," he responded. Anger took over my emotions and I slammed the phone down in his face. Forget Lovely, he's full of himself. It's one thing not to call me after all the messages I left him, but he didn't have to throw her up in my face. And if he really was with her, why did he bother answering the damn phone? According to him, I was the only one with the number to that phone anyway. I hate him! Moving on, I got showered wiping away traces of him from my system, slipped on my favorite jogging suit, grabbed my keys a pad of paper and pencil then took off out the door to my new future.

Hours had passed and I hadn't found anything that I liked. Either the house was nice, but the neighbors weren't or the neighbors were nice and the house wasn't. The asking price for them wasn't too bad, but I wasn't sure if I wanted to spend the next 30 years of my life in a neighborhood heading down hill by next summer. I was looking for a quality home conveniently located home near the main highways of the city with peace and quiet. I didn't have any children, but if and when I did, I desired a safe spot for them to grow up in.

I had to turn in, the sun was going down and I was tired of driving. Besides, I hadn't eaten a thing. I had to be at work in the morning and I needed to wash my uniforms. As soon as I pulled up to my house I noticed Bishop's car at the corner, he wasn't in it. I went on in the house I didn't have anything to say to him. I don't know why he was hanging around, but if I had to, I would call the police on him and send him straight to jail for trespassing, loitering or stalking. The phone was still ringing after I had

Dating My Dad

made it into the house. Whoever it was didn't bother leaving a message. They let it ring a few times, hung up then called back. "Who the hell is this calling like that?" I said. "Hi Momma. I just got in from house hunting. What are you doing up this late?" I said changing my mood. "It's not late Shelby. I'm not a little kid that has to be in bed at a certain hour. Look at here, you really gonna buy a house?" "Yes. I got approved for seventy–five thousand dollars. I figure that should get me something nice, huh?" "Sure, but I want to talk to you about something. I got a better idea that I wanna run by you Shelby," she said, snatching my joy from me as usual. "What's that Momma?" I searched for my cigarettes waiting to hear her better news. "Have you ever thought about purchasing a duplex?" A light bulb went off in my head. I hadn't thought about it, but it wasn't a bad idea at all, not at all. "No Momma, I hadn't, why?" "Well, I love your Auntie Pinkie and everything, but I don't plan on staying here with her forever you know. When you told me you were ready to buy a house I knew that the Lord had answered my prayers, you know?" I lit up my cigarette and took a long drag. "No I don't know what you mean Momma. Are you saying that me working hard and doing something you didn't know that I was going to do was God answering your prayers?" "Well, not like that Shelby. But I've wanted to leave and get my own place, but didn't know where to go or how to go about it. I know I didn't want to go back to that house with your Dad. You and I can get a house together and split the bills, it won't be yours and it won't be mine, it'll be ours. I live up and you live down whichever one you prefer. What do you think about that?" I took another long drag from my cigarette and blew out the smoke with a wheeze. First of all, I don't know if I wanted a duplex and secondly, I didn't know if I wanted to live with Regina. I've lived with her off and on for 18 years and I didn't like that. Thirdly, she could be up to her old games again needing me, but don't want to ask for my help. What does she mean it's not mine or hers, but ours, us didn't get approved, I did. And if something were to happen it would all be on me. That house would be in my name and I would be totally responsible for anything and everything about it. If I were to weigh my options by her history, I would not entertain the thought. When I was thirteen, they (Regina and Spivey) got the electric and gas bill in my name and ran it up to $1300 abusing my name and credit. And when she filed bankruptcy, it never crossed her mind to add my bills to her list of other things to pay off. To this day I have to add my middle initial to my name to get bills in my name. I rigged it so that utility companies and creditors have to contact me before approving me for anything or providing any services.

I thought it would be a good learning experience for me, an easier way of living for Regina and me since the both of us had it hard living with Spivey. I didn't know any better, but I will admit that most of my reasons why was that I felt sorry for Regina because she's my mother, but deep inside I knew I was going to regret having her as my first tenant. Truthfully, I didn't believe she'd appreciate my help, her actions told off on her.

Once I agreed to her plan of us living together in a duplex the next Sunday after she got out of church, we went out house hunting. At first she wanted me to do all of the work, looking and searching, bargaining and buying. I didn't fall for that; I made her come with me so that she wouldn't have anything negative to say, which was my first mistake.

Regina was so annoying and picky. We'd find a decent place in a great location, and then she'd find something wrong with it; anything, like the toilets were too low or too high. I could've pulled all of my hair out from listening to her complain about everything. My approval letter only last 30 days, we had seven days left when we finally decided on this cute two-story bungalow on the Southside of town. It had two bedrooms down and one-bedroom upstairs. It had plenty of yard space wrapped around the house with garage. She argued with me and almost declined it when she noticed that the garage doors had to be opened manually. She's not the buyer, she's the beggar and from what I've always heard, they have no right to be choosy. Regina thought she was the exception to that rule.

Anyway, we searched and found, I offered and closed. Then it was time for us to get on in it and make it our home sweet home. I purchased the home at a steal, but I borrowed an even $60,000 to have emergency money, install an automatic garage door opener, and get some new furniture for my pad. The furniture was a treat for me, but with an old home, you never knew when it would need repairs. Regina surprised me with the new stuff she bought for her place. She had it fixed up really cute for her.

Things were going great for us in the beginning then all of a sudden they changed just like the weather. Regina wanted me to leave my back door open so that she could have access to my house anytime she felt like it. That wasn't all she demanded of me. She hadn't seen the inside of a grocery store since we moved there. Getting the groceries was my job according to her. She wanted me to do the shopping and cooking while she did nothing, not even pay for any of it. What really tripped me out was when autumn came, she refused to turn her gas on to heat her place. "The heat from your house rises up and I don't need the extra bill. I ain't turning no gas on, for what?" She was dead serious; she didn't care if the pipes froze and burst, it wasn't her problem to worry about. She went to work, came home to eat and get ready for church and that was that.

Speaking of her going to church; one day she got under my skin. Her words lingered and crawled inside me once she told me that she didn't have her side of the mortgage to pay. "I don't have it! I didn't ask you for rent while I carried you nine and a half months, did I!" she screamed at me from her back door. I wasn't trying to hear that. "What am I supposed to tell the mortgage company? My mother can't pay me so I can't pay y'all this month," she lost her mind and I was losing mine too. I shut my door and locked her out. "Things gonna change around here. I promise you that." I mumbled on as if she was there to hear me. What was she doing with her money that she didn't have it to pay her responsibilities? Beliefs of her giving it to the church crept into my mind shifting my entire outlook on her new church home. What kind of place of worship was this that she had to pay to attend? From what I read and heard, God only required 10% of your increase not everything you needed to survive on. Nevertheless, I would soon find out. I got dressed and waited for the van to pick her up and I trailed them about 5 miles north to 29th Street where the church sat in the middle of the block. I was posted waiting for the van full of churchgoers to get out and go in. I sat a few more minutes until I heard music, and then I rolled up the window, got out of my car and locked the doors. I ran across the street and opened the door and walked right on in. "Welcome and God bless you sister," said a very tall, nice man who greeted me. "Thank you sir," I said back bashfully. I had every intention of going in that church and exposing them and her with the truth instead I got lured in and ushered in a seat in the front row. The choir sang the most beautiful song I had ever heard. They were clapping and rocking side-to-side so cheerful that a warm feeling came over me. This feeling had me thinking I was closer to God just because I was there. I stood up alongside with others and joined in on the joy that flowed throughout the sanctuary. By the time they were half way through the second song, tears formed and rolled down my face. I was cleansed of all my guilt and sin, I knew it because they didn't know me from a hill of poop and there they were singing my personal pains from my body. "The Lord knows," they sung. I cried some more. It must have been an answered prayer because when my eyes found Regina up on the podium, she was in tears too. Next thing I knew the pastor had his arms around me praying then the music stopped and the worshippers prayed with him. "Little lady do you believe that God loves you?" he asked me while putting the old taped together microphone up to my mouth. "Yes, I believe," I said as I sobbed. "He's asking you to come closer to Him and surrender yourself to Him and trust Him. Will you trust Him? He's waiting for you." "Where is He sir, I want to go to Him?" "He's right here, He's everywhere and if you want He will always be with you." He held open his arms to me for a hug. I did, and then I cried like a baby as the pastor embraced me. My soul felt renewed, my heart didn't ache as much feeling this man's arms wrapped around me like I was his daughter. I hadn't had anyone that I could remember love on me like he was. I cried some more. My embarrassment left me alone to absorb the love. I wiped away my tears with a handkerchief that the pastor had given me from his blazer. He held my hand gently and walked me over to the side into the back of the church to a nurse that was waiting with a cold glass of water. "Give God a hand you all, praise God that could've been your daughter, mother, sister or relative you've been praying for to see the Lord move in their life like He moved in that young lady's life. She was in pain and she is on the way to a full recovery. Praise the Lord of all lords, Jesus our Savior." Inside the back there were other nurses and deacons praying with others that were weeping.

I straightened up to drink the rest of my water, then smiled signaling that I was better and ready to go back into the church with the rest of the congregation. My questions had been answered. I wasn't being selfish, but I was interested in hearing Pastor Cross preach. I sat back attentively and enjoyed the sermon. Now I realized why Regina had chosen Urban Affair Full Gospel Baptist Church as her new church home. It was the love that they shared and the clear easy learning of God. Regina was in a lot of pain too, and in need of love to make her better. Craig told me that God loves people who are in pain and children, even adult children. And there were a lot of little people there rejoicing right alongside of us, made me wish I had been raised up in church with a better perceptive of this love that filled me. I loved to be happy from the inside out, not the outside in, just like them kids I witnessed that night in their sincerity.

The morning was bright, I pulled the curtains back and rolled the blinds open to let the sunrays come on in and light up the kitchen table and warm up the seats as I brewed some coffee for Regina and me. I cracked my back door to let the aroma hike the steps straight to her bedroom up her nose to wake her up and bringing her on downstairs. I had a seat on the couch observing the view, admiring my new home and the style I came up with. The earth-toned furniture and soft pink painted walls gave the home a soothing feel. The warm spirit lingered causing me to discover the true meaning of relaxation, made me glad to get up and go to work every day. My bedroom was exotic and romantic at the same time. I put together soft pink and black trim wall colors surrounding my extra-large black leather platform waterbed. The pillows were plush and soft. I loved that bed, in the summer it was cool to lay on and in the winter it was warm. Though plenty of people complained of motion sickness with waterbeds, I didn't have a problem. I loved it, for my age, I was doing well and I knew it.

Anyway, I put my feet in some slippers when I heard the door swing open. Just like I thought, the coffee woke Regina up. She was bright eyed with a big smile on her face. "Good morning Momma, have a seat I'll fix you a cup," I returned the smile. "Good morning Shelby, you up early. Ain't you off today?" she asked as she scratched her forearm and wiped her mouth. "I'm off Momma, but I got up early this morning feeling good from last night. I really enjoyed myself. I'm glad I went." I said as I reached over her for a coffee cup in the cupboard. I wanted to hug her, but the vibe told me to get the cup and keep moving. "Oh yeah Shelby, what made you show up last night? I didn't expect you there." "Momma I...I had something on my mind that was eating me up so I followed you to the place where you get your help. I wasn't spying on you." I gave her half the truth. The reason I went wasn't as major as the reasons I stayed. "Everybody was talking about how beautiful you are and they didn't know my daughter was so big. They must've thought I had a little girl instead of a grown daughter. I don't talk to them too much you gotta keep folks out of your business no matter where you meet them. By the way, don't be telling them none of my business Shelby," she made eye contact with me making sure I understood. "Momma, why would I do that? I didn't say that I would be going there on a regular. Last night was my first time and probably my last, but I enjoyed it, that's all," I responded. I couldn't believe she said that. It was if she had something to hide. Regina has been a handful lately. She's been complaining and whining about everything. She probably missed Spivey. She had never been without him that long. The separation could be taking a toll on her. After all, she was his programmed, codependent. In my opinion, she was doing just fine. Regina and Auntie Pinkie have been hanging out doing girly stuff, shopping and going out to dinner like women their ages should be doing, enjoying life to the fullest. I knew Regina was not use to being with anyone else but Spivey, but if she could only see things from my point. She needed to keep up the good work. Though we didn't get along that well, I loved seeing her free and unattached. I prayed that she could hang in there a little while longer and he'll be out of her system. It's not easy detaching yourself from someone that you've been with just about forever and a day.

Just when I thought things were getting better between Regina and I, she had to go and pull crazy lady out on me again. All I did was ask her for some money on the electric bill. She hadn't had her electricity since we moved in three months ago. She does everything that requires heat and electricity downstairs in my home. I didn't know what made her flip out on me. I was asking a normal question that anyone would have asked considering our set up. I never agreed with her using me, but I never told her no, I assumed asking her to help me help her was reasonable, but I guess not. "Shelby, let me tell you something. I see what you're doing! You trying to take advantage of me just like you tried to do when I was with Spivey and he wasn't around. You need to stop acting like the devil and stay with Jesus!" She looked at me as if I would say another word to her she would scratch my eyes out. I remained silent, thinking of what I was going to do to stop her from taking advantage of me. "I'ma lock my doors and that will be that." I whispered. I couldn't restrain myself. I was not going to let her get away with her game, mother or not. It wasn't fair and she knew it. I could've been wrong, but I don't know anyone trying to make it that would pay for their mother's way when she could take care of herself. "What did you say? You think you're grown now and can talk to me any kinda way Shelby?" Regina walked up on me with those blood shot red eyes trying to intimidate me. She did and I stepped back to turn around. Next thing I knew she was throwing any and everything she could pick up at me. Regina called me everything but a child of God. She was acting possessed like the devil himself. I retreated to my room closed and locked the door. Regina banged on the door repeatedly for me to open it, but I was reluctant. Truthfully, I was afraid of her and terrified of what would happen if I opened the door. So I left her out there screaming and bashing me.

"Momma stop, this is insane and uncaused for. Please Momma calm down. You are tripping out and if you don't stop I'ma call the police on you and have you removed." I heard a big thump. I jumped up and opened the door Regina was laid out on the carpet breathing heavily. "Momma, what's wrong with you? Are you okay? Get up." I panicked discovering my mother spread out on the floor. I ran into the kitchen to get her some water. When I returned, she was covered in sweat and shaking all over. "Momma, what's wrong?" "I don't know, it's hot as hell in here, but I feel cold." She responded. I couldn't handle seeing her like that anymore. I ran to the phone and dialed 911.

No wonder Regina had been acting so weird lately. It turned out that she was going through menopause. I learned from the doctors what menopause was all about and I felt sorry for Regina, but that still didn't justify her long and rough treatment towards me. Especially now when I was being the perfect daughter to her despite the past. I asked if multiple personalities came with the change because she's was two-faced as a person could come. Regina was kinder to her church friends than she was to her only child. I mean when no one was looking she was cruel to me, at her own free will. And what did I do to cause her to snap out on me, was anybody's guess. What I do know is that I can't carry all the weight alone when I was looking out for the both of us. What sense would that make? It's a shame, but I almost understood why Spivey mistreated her all of those years, in a way, she deserved it. She gave him the remote control and he changed her channels whenever he felt like it.

I thank God she was spending the night at Auntie Pinkie's house. I needed to think things over and come up with a game plan. With the way things have been going, we won't be living together much longer. It started out as a good thing, but it takes at least two people, to be a team. And Regina's got to be willing to do her part. "I didn't charge you rent when I carried you nine months in my belly? You didn't have to pay for the damages to my body that you caused me either," she said into my ears into my mind. Sticks and stones do break your bones and cruel words from a loved one can break your spirit. Regina was full of anger with me. I tried to look over them and sympathize with her for the abuse she endured. But it was hard since she wasn't sympathetic of my pain. I came from the same abusive situation as she by the same man and now that we were free, she tried to keep us both there; no thank you. I'm staying free of the mental kill no matter what I have to do even if I had to get rid of her.

"Well would you tell Momma that I love her please?" I asked of Auntie Pinkie. I called over there to check up on Regina and apologize to her for whatever I did to cause her to snap. Truth be told, I wanted to keep the peace and go on with life without all of the bitterness and resentment. "She'll be fine Shelby. Don't worry about your momma. Pray for her and pray for Spivey. The Lord says we are to pray for our enemies. He's been calling her all day. She must've spoken with him and let him know she was over here. She was smiling when she got off the phone with him." Auntie Pinkie instructed me. "When did Dad get home? I haven't heard from him since I left him at the hospital." I was concerned myself. "Out the hospital, Shelby honey, he's back in there and he might not make it out of there this time around. He needs a liver transplant." I searched my purse for a cigarette and my lighter. *"Spivey wasn't going to be satisfied until he killed himself,"* I thought to myself. "Auntie Pinkie do you know what they did to dad to bring him back to normal again?" I asked in disbelief that he would ever look at another liquor bottle again. "He's sick Auntie Pinkie, he's sick," I said as tears formed and rolled down my face. Spivey still had control over my mother and me. I don't care who the person is, when you love them, I mean really love a person, love don't disappear because they are suffering. If you care a little you'll end up suffering with them because you care, maybe more about them than they care for themselves. And instead of them going down the drain alone, they expect loved ones to go down the drain for them or if not for them, with them. "Auntie Pinkie, I'ma do everything in my power to stop my mother from going back to the hell hole he had her trapped in most of her life," I took a long drag of my cigarette as I paced the floors. My skin itched at the thought of Regina giving in to him, leaving what's been good to her. "She's too old, she's too damn old. Excuse my language Auntie Pinkie." "You're all right Baby. I understand. I'm upset too. But there's really nothing we can do but pray right now and hope for the best. I'ma get off this phone and make sure your mother is comfortable. You get some rest for work my niece and I promise to pray for you all tonight and I will call you when I think you're home from work, me love you." "Thank you and me love you too." I loved talking to Auntie Pinkie she always knew what to say and what to do. I felt things would be fine. I got off the phone and turned on the radio to the soft jazz station, ran me some hot water in the tub, got in and relaxed.

Episode 14

Summer of 1992

Dating My Dad

From the outside looking in, you would guess that I was doing well. I got a raise from my job, which let up more money to save and I would have been, but I caught the Jones'. I was spending like crazy; I acted like I have never had anything before. Truthfully, I hadn't ever had it this good and it showed. My house was decked out in every room with no room left to put anything, but it was clutter free. I had every appliance a woman could want that the new Wal-Mart Super Store offered. You would have thought Martha Stewart paid me a few visits the way I organized things. My bedroom was a playgirl's dream, full of pink Playboy bunnies and pictures of sexy men. After I furnished my living room and dining room, I went out into the back hallway, then out the door to the backyard. I had the most pleasant backyard. I could see Lovely and me having cook-outs and cocktails back there. Anyway, I wasn't a green thumb holder like my elder neighbor, but as far as decorating, I could hang with her. I figured by next summer I'd learn a few tricks to the trade of gardening from her and have myself a slice of that joyful pie she seems to have every time I see her out there grooming her yard and picking her choice of vegetables. For now, mine fit me, very low maintenance, all I have to do is cut and water the grass and edge it up a bit. I didn't stop there; I went around the side, putting different sized pink and white rocks against the house to match with the motion sensitive lights that lit up as you approached them. They were stylish plus they added a little security. I had an entrance gate installed on the side to keep people from trespassing. Regina liked that a lot because she mostly entered through the back. "That way people stay out of your business, they don't see when you come or when you leave. If something were to happen, they ain't going to claim to see anything anyway, so why do they need to know your comings and goings?" she reprimanded.

    I finished up my last project, the sun porch a few days before summer hit and to my surprise, it was beautiful. It looked like a whole new different house. I set it up like an African Safari with surreal looking tall plants covering the windows blocking some of the blazing sun. Regina turned her nose up when she first saw it, but she had been coming down and having coffee with me and we eased from the kitchen to the sunroom at her call. She said I should've had a house warming party, but I didn't want to get stuff from people that I wasn't going to put to use. Besides, I was in control and wanted to do things my way while I had the opportunity trying to show her the life she and I both could've had if she would've heard me out the first time I asked. She's my mother and she wanted to be in charge. Whether she liked it or not, I felt complete now that I had the house finished in time for summer fun. I have a new looking car too. I took a few hundred dollars and got my Nova repainted and the man cleaned it up nicely, like a sports car. The only thing left for me to do was to buy me some new threads, which is what I've been doing for a few days. I ventured off to major department stores and the outlets, shopping away until I spiffed up my wardrobe. I won't have to wear the same outfit for months to come. When Lovely sees me he's going to faint. I finally got myself all together and polished up. All that I had to do was maintain what I had and enjoy my season of happiness. Best of all I don't start back up in school until the fall. This has been my year. No more Bishop, I got a new house, new ride, everything I've pretty much ever wanted except Lovely in my corner. Maybe he'll come around when he sees me and my new home with the new attitude to match. He better act right or else, let the other entertainment began. Regina didn't approve of my new friend girl Desiree, but I liked her, she was level headed and from what I see at work, we have a lot in common. She kept to herself and stayed out of the realm of garbage that is commonly circulated whenever there are a lot of women working together. We were on the same shift and partnered up a lot because we both hated dragging the day. We'd get our work done early and hang out in the women's bathroom or in one of our patients' rooms at the last hour of our shift waiting to punch out. We sat down together in the cafeteria a few times for lunch. I went out with her and we had a ball, she was the same spunky person outside of work. The way I see it, when you work with people forty hours or more a week, you spend at least 80% of your time around them, way too much energy spent for putting up a facade. At some point in time the real you had got to come out. My mother had two female friends in her circle and she didn't want more than that in my circle either, but Desiree was cool people in my book. Regina just had to get to know her. Like I said, we had a lot in common, she was a go-getter like me and she didn't stand for any chaos. Though we worked at a nursing home as C.N.A.'s with a bunch of women, there were only a few messy ones at Saint Claire's and they hung together wishing they were us.

Anyway, Desiree wanted me to go out with her to meet this guy that she met over the phone, Keep-in-Touch Hotline, an adult social hotline. I thought of it as strange that she would have to stoop to that level of meeting someone. I saw the commercial for the phone line, I also had seen the physic hotline, but I wasn't going to pick up the phone and call it. Desiree was gorgeous and could have any man that laid eyes on her on any street in Milwaukee, but she was different and wanted something more than average I guess. It wasn't like she did this all the time this was her first time. I was open-minded, but I had limits. I agreed to go with her for her safety plus I wanted to see the results for myself; I might try it if she snags someone worth it. I was more excited about going than she was. "What's wrong Desiree, you don't want to see him face to face now?" I asked staring at her through the restroom mirror as she refreshed her face. "I'm okay Shelby, it's just that he sounds so good and intelligent over the phone and all, but he might be fat and ugly and on top of all of that broke. I don't have time for that. You just don't know nowadays. I can tell you this because you are my gurl Shelby; I've gotten attached to him. He has a strong personality and he's very smart," she said to me. "Is he from here?" I asked as a pink flag went up in my head. "Yes, but he moved away then just got back a few months ago," another flag went up; I put my hand up to my chest to catch my breath. "What is his name? Please don't tell me Bishop Styles?" she asked as she turned to me with a surprised look on her face. "No Shelby, his name is Mark Gives. You know I know all about Mr. Styles and first of all I don't do that. I wouldn't date anyone you've talked to. And secondly, did you forget the shit you told me about that trifling ass con artist? I will slap him whenever or if ever I see him for the shit he pulled with you!" I smiled in relief. "I'm sorry Dezie. I know better. I wasn't thinking. Forgive me sweetie. You are my dog." "Shut up Shelby. I love you Gurl. Let's get the hell out of here, we've been here for two hours, it's time to get the hell out of here," she said as she checked her watch. "I'm with that," I replied. We left the meeting spot, gathered our things, punched out and left.

Not bad at all, he was a bit taller than Desiree, brown skinned and handsome, very distinguished. His presence could not go unnoticed. I went back to the table to give Desiree the okay. "He looks good?" she asked in a surprised tone. Desiree hopped out of the booth seat hurrying over to greet him. I opened my laminated menu to see what I wanted. The waitress came with waters and asked if I was ready to order. I looked down at the menu to choose between a spinach pizza or meat lovers. "Can I have a few more minutes please; I'm waiting for my sister to return?" "No thanks, we're leaving." Desiree interrupted, "What do you mean Desiree? Where's your date?" I asked as my eyes bucked. I know we have different taste in men, but I thought he was okay for a blind date. "Gurl come with me to the spot," I grabbed my purse and water trailing her to the restroom. Desiree checked the stalls to make sure we were alone. "Shelby?" she put her hands on her hips and leaned hard to the right. "Shelby?" "Yes," I responded in anticipation of what went down. "Shelby you said he looked good?" "Well, he did for a blind date. He wasn't no dog-face, he looked decent to me. He is clean cut and better than average. I've seen some better and a ton of worse. What did you think?" I answered with a confused look on my face. "*Was I that off?*" I thought to myself. I know Desiree likes the finer things in life, but he wasn't bad at all. It wasn't like someone she knows set her up with him; they met over the phone on a hotline. He could've been ugly. It just isn't like a nice looking man to be on a hotline trying to meet somebody when he could meet women the good old-fashion way average men do every day. "Shelby, he looked good on the outside until he smiled. Oh my God, Shelby he didn't have any teeth. Not a one." I couldn't hold it in; I burst out laughing, "Get out of here Desiree. No teeth at all?" I didn't catch that. "Hell naw, he didn't have any teeth to chew. What was he going to do at dinner?" We both broke out laughing. That would explain why he held his head down when he smiled. "What did you do Desiree?" she asked as she held her stomach as she laughed some more. "I told him I wasn't interested at all. He took right off. And that's the end of that. He should've told me that over the phone. That's important news you just don't leave out you know?" "I feel you on that, but what about the long talks you and him been having? Does that count for anything?" she laughed again, "Shelby I don't have time to be falling in love just to get right back out of love with somebody I know I'm not going to be happy with forever. He got to at least have a cute smile." We laughed and left the bathroom. I was glad to make it to the car. I understood where Desiree was coming from, but the paranoia of what he would do being rejected like that kept me checking the area. I hoped she wasn't the first woman to turn him down quick the way she did. She didn't really know him and neither did I. He could be a stalker or worse for all we knew.

I called Lovely's car phone eight times and still no answer, I had to have one of Desiree's men friends give me a jump. I came into work early and forgot to shut off my lights. I was grateful that he gave me a boost, but I was embarrassed when he asked me where my man was to help me. "Hell your guess is as good as mine. He must be busy because I did call him, but he didn't answer." "Did you leave him a message?" he asked looking into my eyes as if I hadn't thought of that. "Yes, but he hasn't paged me or called up here yet. I will pay you for your troubles and let him know what happened today, thank you so much." "No problem. You

Dating My Dad

don't have to pay me. I love doing whatever to get with Desiree. I love that girl with all my heart, but she's too independent. But she ain't got to lift a finger doing no manly stuff as long as I'm around," he smiled. I returned the smile thinking how much he cared for Desiree and she really didn't want him. Maybe if I treated Lovely the way she treats her man, he would take a big gulp of some act-right too.

Anyway, he put his red positive cable on the plus side of his battery and the black grip on the negative side on his battery. I watched the entire process. Then he put the other red positive cable on the positive side of my battery and the black grip onto the minus sign side of my battery. "Get in your car and start it up," he instructed me. I opened the door, got in, turned the key, and it cranked up. I put the biggest grin on my face. He gave me the thumbs up, snatched the cables off both of our vehicles and closed the hoods. "Let me know if you need any help with your car again. I'd be happy to help. I fix cars too, and Nova's are my favorite. I got a homeboy named Bryce that works at the auto parts garage on 83rd and Greenfield. He'll give you a good price on anything you need. Let him know Greg sent you." "What do I owe you Greg?" "You don't owe me anything. I was leaving to come this way when Desiree called me anyway. You have a good one," he smiled. "Thank you," I said and waved letting my car run a bit before I took off. When I get to the house I'ma call up Lovely's phone and beeper until he responds. I don't know what's gotten into him or who has gotten a hold of him, but it's not like him not to call me. I will have to step out and see him face to face and let him have a piece of my mind. Anyway the words Greg said to me crossed my mind about his friend working at the auto parts store. I do want to get some new designer mud flaps and floor rugs for my ride. I punched the accelerator while turning left onto the highway going West about 4 miles, and then I exited at Greenfield Avenue to the right searching for the place.

Once inside I noticed a slab of handsome young men behind the counter. When I say handsome, I meant handsome. All shades of brown, medium height to very tall, soft voices too deep and heavy, but fine as all outdoors. I was nervous and it showed. My mouth watered like I had eaten a ripe tangerine. As I patiently waited for my turn to ask for Bryce my eyes wandered around as if I was patrolling the area trying to match the name with a face. I was hoping he was this tall cutie that I seemed to keep staring at me. "Can I help you ma'am?" one of them asked me, but it wasn't the one I was staring at however he was just as good looking. I wiped my chin in fear that there might be some drool. "Umm, I'm looking for Bryce?" I asked in my schoolteacher tone. "He's off today; can I help you with something?" I flipped my hair out of my eye flirting with all of them. "Umm, no thank you. He was recommended to me. Do you know when he'll be in?" "No I don't, but I can help you with something if you like. I'm the assistant manager to Bryce." *"Did he just wink at me?"* I thought to myself. I put a shy grin on my face, "I'll just come back. Do you know when he'll be in please?" "Let me check his schedule for you." He stepped down from the counter and I like to have fallen out. This man was a brick house that walked like he owned the isles. I watched him too, like a hawk watches prey. "Are you a nurse?" another cutie pie asked of me interrupting my naughty thoughts. "Are you a nurse?" he repeated. I flipped my hair again giving myself a head rush. "Something like that. Why?" "Your scrubs are all white and you don't have a speck of dirt on you," he explained. "Thank you I guess, but I'm a nurse's assistant." "How do you like doing that? I was going to do that, but they changed my hours here and you know the rest," he gave. I took a closer look at him after I noticed him flipping his hand down while talking to me. The thought of him being gay dropped down and landed in front of my face. "You can always get a job doing this. They're in high demand. Maybe you can do it another time?" I told him. "Yeah, you right. I'm tired of this place. I hate getting dirty and staying dirty. Some nights I go home and I scrub and scrub," he finished. The assistant manager came back into the area. "Ma'am, he's off until Wednesday morning. Would you like to leave a message?" "Umm, you can just tell him Shelby came by and I'll catch up with him later. Oh yeah, tell him that Greg sent me to see him." "Okay. I'll let him know you stopped by. Have a good day." "Thank you." I wanted to stay, but I had to leave. The auto store had emptied and I was about to be in the hot seat. I felt like I was looking a hot mess, but they didn't care. I was the only female in sight. I waved good-bye to all that could see me and put a little more twitch in my hips as I walked away. I laughed at the boys lining up to get a glimpse of me. I heard the murmuring about who I was. I hopped in the Nova, fast forward my cassette to the next cut by Prince, turned it up and drove off. The store wasn't too far from the house I could swing by next week. It wasn't a priority for me to have those things for my car yet. But to lift my spirits, I could think of something I'd need for my car every payday in order to go in there. I was curious to know what Bryce looked like.

Two days after my car stopped Lovely finally called me. He gave the lamest excuse I'd ever heard for not answering my calls. "My people was with me." He knows I knew better than that, but what could I say. He does have a live-in significant other. Still, it was something fishy going on with him. He didn't even sound the same. He sounded distant like he was giving me the cold shoulder. Maybe the good times were over between us. I wanted to tell him about the house and everything that's been going on in my life, but he didn't ask me anything or seem interested in knowing anything. Though I couldn't handle his rejection or mistreatment, I held on to the good that we shared. I was connected to him more than my emotions could control. Seems he could care less. Truth be told, I was tired of lying to people trying to paint this perfect picture of another failed relationship with a man. According to me, we were doing fine. I lied about him calling me so much that he actually stopped. The only person other than me that knew the truth was Regina and she didn't care one bit. She didn't want me with anyone anyhow; she liked the freedom that she had with me. As long as nobody was there, she did what she wanted to do. But what I didn't understand was how she turned into the daughter and me the mother.

It was bizarre to see Pat's packed that late in the evening. I drug Desiree out with me to have a few cocktails and sneak up on Lovely. At first I rode pass to make sure his car was there. It was and I damn near left my car running with the doors unlocked to get inside. I really didn't care if Desiree sensed my desperation I was trying to catch Lovely in the act. My suspicions told me that somebody other than his significant other caught his eye causing him to kick me to the curb. His woman was there way before I came along so it wouldn't be her sucking up his attention. The only tie that they had was the one she got in his ear when he first fell in love with her easing her, way into his home. Now all that was left was his morals that won't let him put her out for someone else. If you ask me, she's stupid for putting up with his mess that long. If he was mine all mine, I'd have a tight leash around him holding the short strap so close that all he could do is take a squat, sit or lay down like the dog he was.

It crushed me not to see Lovely in sight. From what I heard, he had left out not too long before I arrived. I was told to stay put and don't go anywhere. "Have a few and sit tight," Doug demanded. He took a liking to me the first time we were introduced, but he was loyal because he wouldn't out a word of Lovely's whereabouts. If anyone knew where Lovely was it would be him and Ms. Juicy Juice. Anyway, Desiree was comfortable and enjoying the home feel of the bar. She and Ms. Juicy Juice had a few friendly words in between drinks. "Ms. Juicy Juice, don't forget who your baby is," I joked. I was glad they welcomed Desiree. "You know I know who my baby is. What else do you want to drink Little Lovely?" "Please make me something special as long as it gets the job done." I smiled holding up my half-full glass of Strawberry Daiquiri. "Shelby isn't this place where you and Lovely hangout at?" Desiree snooped. "Yeah, this is the place. Why; do you like it?" she asked as she finished off her Blueberry Daiquiri. "I like it a lot. It's like the TV show Cheers, everybody knows your name. And you have a great time with some good smelling food." "The food is good too. Wait until you have the chicken wings and fries. You're going to come back for more trust me." "Oh yeah." "Yeah," we said to each other over the loud music.

I kept checking the door for Lovely, no sign; he might have seen my car and kept going. Just as I thinking of him, and then in walked one of his other buddies. "What's happening Shelby Baby?" I turned around in my chair because I recognized the voice. "Hey Baby where you been?" I asked and a big smile formed on my face. It was Lovely he was hiding behind his friend as they entered Pat's. He was grinning from ear to ear. You would've thought everything was fine with the way he pretended nothing was out of order with us. For the sake of peace, I played it off too, though I was tempted to slap him at any moment. If I got drunk enough and the opportunity came, I just might have seized the offer. I introduced Desiree to Lovely and of course he put the charm on thick. "You favor my Shelby Baby. Y'all sisters or related somehow?" he asked after I introduced her as my co-worker and friend. I gave him a quick *stop-showing-out* glance. "Whats up Shelby Baby, come show me how much you missed me?" he straightened up. He wanted me to do our public greeting ritual. I didn't. I smiled and flirted with his friend to let him know how it felt to have somebody you care about being flirtatious with someone else in your face. Lovely taught me how to have the upper hand and I kept it. He couldn't come into my life spoiling me and showing me the finer things in life all to snatch the blankets off me and disrespect me when he chose. I couldn't handle not being on his list of champions. I wasn't a loser.

Desiree ordered another drink, but Lovely's buddy jumped in to pay for the rest of them, if she wanted. "My name is Milk and I'm health to your bones and good for your soul." Milk put a huge smile on his face. I could tell Desiree dug his flavor. She giggled and agreed. I was relieved to see them getting along. Thank God she wasn't like Addison too precious and snappy, so complicated that you didn't know what her problem was.

Taking her out was like caring for a 9-month-old baby, one minute everything's fine and peaceful. The next, you were running around trying to figure out what to do to stop the baby from whining and screaming at the top of its lungs. Nevertheless, Desiree showed maturity, if she liked Milk or not, she was cool enough for me to enjoy myself even if she was uncomfortable. So I was able to dip off into a corner to talk with Lovely. I needed to feel him out, find out what was going on in that big head of his. I wanted the truth about his distance from me. I wanted to know what was really distracting him. Truth be told, I could handle truth at any time.

"That's it Lovely, that's all you had to say to me for being away from me so long?" "What do you want me to say? I've been with my people! I can't help it. I have crisis too. You're tripping Shelby," I leaned back and gave him an awkward look. "Shelby?" he rolled his eyes back as he patted his shirt pocket for a lighter to smoke his cigar. "That's your name ain't it?" he spewed and I exhaled. I didn't want to go into detail with him about his sarcasm; he knew he was acting up calling me Shelby. Ever since the day I met Lovely my name has been Shelby Baby. "Okay Lovely, you win. I don't want to fight with you or get on the wrong side with you right now. I'm disturbed because I haven't seen you in a while and I miss you much more than you understand." I hoped my words penetrated that thick head of his turning his heart back into the direction it was a few weeks ago. "Stop tripping off small things Shelby. I got you, you're still my ace. As long as I'm alive you always got a friend in me." I missed seeing that gold trimmed tooth shining before me. "Well, I got so much to tell you and I hadn't had the opportunity to share it with you that's all. You know?" I leaned forward to kiss his soft juicy lips. He met me in the middle and our lips touch, but his wasn't anywhere near as soft as they usually were. I kissed on him again anyway. He wasn't perfect at all and neither was I. Besides, I have always believed when you love somebody, if you pay attention to every little negative thing, you'll end up overlooking a lump of love. "Go ahead and talk, my guy is cool and your girl is straight too. Where you meet her? How old is she? She thick and fine." *"Damn, let me pull out her birth certificate and hand it to him so he'll know everything about her,"* I thought to myself. "Watch it Lovely! You know I don't play that. For your information again, I told you that I work with her. She's old enough to do what she wants without a legal guardian. Do you want me to go get her for you?" I put my elbows on the table holding up my head to show my frustrations with him being out of line. "See there, you jealous. I can't joke around with you for you getting all serious." He puffed his cigar and blew out the smoke into my face. My eyes watered and my nose twitched. "You damn right, I'm serious. That's some foul shit. I wouldn't play with you like that. I don't find you being disrespectful funny," he said as he reached over to me with open arms. "Okay Shelby Baby, take it easy Gurl. I still love you. You love me?" he cracked. "Sometimes," I cracked back. "Awh right tell me all about what's been going on with my Shelby Baby," I took a deep breath of relief that he was interested and began telling him what's been going on in my life, blabbing away about my new house. Lovely's eyes swelled at my accomplishments. I was excited to be sharing my dreams with someone that knew what it was like to have been deprived as a child.

 In the back of my head something squirmed forward warning me of the distance between us. It was as if Lovely didn't like the idea of me

Dating My Dad

being on the same level as him at my young age. What could I do? Technically he wasn't my man so I had to take care of myself. "Good for you Ms. Shelby. Good for you Baby," he rudely interrupted me holding up his hand to catch the waitress's attention. She came over to the booth. "Whatcha need Lovely?" "Give her what she wants and bring me a bottle of Imperator." What did he mean, whatever she wants, he knows I drink what he drinks and he knows I love me some Imperator. I couldn't stomach his fake attitude. He wasn't happy for me and I could feel it. Truth was, I was in love with Lovely, but I was just a pass time for him. I held on enough for Desiree to exchange digits with Milk and enjoy her time there, then we took off. I kissed Lovely like it was the last time I'd be seeing him. I hoped he'd opens his eyes and rekindle the flame we once had, but until then I decided that night to give him his space. I could be there if he wanted, but he'd have to leave clues he wanted me to follow.

At the beginning of the year Desiree and I put in to have the Fourth of July weekend off and were granted that plus the following Monday and Tuesday was our regular scheduled time off. We planned to drive up to Minnesota and see the Mall of America and shop until we ran out of money. Desiree offered to rent a car, but I suggested we take my ride for the trip, not only to save money for more shopping, but the Nova needed a long highway road trip anyway.

I cleaned up the house really good and restocked groceries for Regina. I was packed and anxious to get going when Lovely asked if I had my oil changed and a tune up first. "No. I didn't think I needed to." "You need to have it checked before you hit the road Shelby Baby." "Okay, I will," I answered and got off the phone with him. He didn't want to go with us, but he could've at least had my ride inspected for me since he knew it all. I had been feeding him with a long handle spoon; getting hurt by him or any other man wasn't in my future plans. Lovely was going to have to choose what he wanted to do with me. He could either let me be, leave me alone or put me back on top, nothing else would be acceptable to me. I know he has someone else, but I didn't ask him to mess with me in the first place. I can feel him drifting away from me and he's probably feeling obligated to stick around. If he would just gain the heart to say it, I'll be out of his life and out of his way so he could be free to mingle some more.

I gave Regina all the numbers I had for her to get in touch with me if she needed to. She claimed she wasn't going to be in the house all weekend because she had some things lined up. If it wasn't church, work, or my Auntie Pinkie's house, Regina didn't have a life. I know she's going to be home all weekend professing to be starving because she wouldn't cook anything. That's why I picked out mostly snacks and junk foods that I knew she loved. Knowing her the way I do, if it's got my name on it, she won't have any problem taking it, eating it up and apologizing later. "When you coming back?" she asked as I rolled my luggage up to the back door. "We'll be back Tuesday evening. Are you going to be okay alone Momma?" She put her hand on her hip and leaned hard to the right. At least I know where I got that from. "Shelby pu-lease. I'm your Momma and solitary is good for the soul. I'ma get me some rest and get prayed up around here, re-bless the house, get them devils out of here and praise the Lord. Don't you worry about me, you're the one going out where the demons are and I'ma pray you don't bring none back here with you." I shook my head and smiled at Regina. I was amazed at her strength. I remembered I use to be afraid to leave her alone for the weekend in fear of her going back to Spivey. She's stronger than I considered she'd be. God is good to her and He listens to prayers. I hope the Lord fixes Lovely and me. "I love you Momma. I'll be right back, I have to make a run to get the car checked before I hit the road." "Okay, I'm going upstairs to shower, make sure I see you before you head out." "Okay, by the time you get done, I should be back." I watched her go up the stairs, then I headed out the back to the garage.

I pulled into the parking lot with my windows down and my car stereo cassette player booming a new single by Loose Ends as loud as my sounds could go. I caught some dudes peeping out from the store to see who was pulling up playing goodies. I stalled for a few letting my music fill the airways while gathering my purse and inspecting my make-up and hair at the same time before getting out of the car. The garage was full of handsome eligible men, not the kind of place a woman would want to get caught slipping on her beauty. I put a slow groove to my walk like confidence was my best friend. I stood about 5'5" tall, but I glided like I was 6 feet tall on a runway modeling for Used Jeans. I spoke kindly to an older man vacating the store. "Damn!" One of them let out as he passed by me. I giggled and entered. I didn't remember it being that many hunks in there the last time. It felt like I was in the cereal aisle at the grocery store with all of my favorite brands in front of me to choose from. "You're looking for Bryce right?" the assistant manager asked of me. He gave me the warmest welcoming smile. "No not this time, but if he's here I'd like to meet him face-to-face," "All right, let me get him for you," I snatched at my shirt making sure it wasn't twisted. Oh my goodness, the man behind him approaching me was so fine I almost fell out. He was taller than most of them at the store and a crispy brown color complexion with red like he had a trace of Indian blood in his genetic stream somewhere. His legs were thick and bowed a touch; I couldn't help but to stare at him. I was gawking so hard that I jumped when he spoke. "Are you all right?" "Ah, yes, I'm fine. I was trying to remember what I'm supposed to be getting from here. Hello Bryce, I'm Shelby Spivey, nice to meet you," I held out my hand for him to shake it. I really wanted him to bend down and kiss it gently. "Do I know you?" he asked looking surprised that I knew his name. "Umm, no you don't, Greg referred me to you." "Oh Greg, yeah, he's always sending people in here after me. How can I help you today?" Finally, he shook my hand. He seemed relieved that somebody sent me. As cute as he was I knew he had to be a player. Truth be told, he's too young for me. I liked them older than me. "I need my oil and tires check for my road trip. Do y'all do that here?" I asked crushing the thoughts of me being with him. I really need to get it together. I was still working on Lovely's ugly self, I didn't need another headache. "I can take a look at it for you if you like Ms...what was your name again?" "Shelby Spivey." Why I gave him my full name twice, was anybody's guess? I usually don't for my protection. These days you never knew who would get pulled over by the cops and use your name and spell it all wrong, but you'd still receive the ticket for it until you could clear your name. Regina and Spivey scarred me for life using my name for things I didn't do.

Anyway, I waited quietly for him to get the tools he needed, then he led the way out of the door to have a look at my car. According to him I was ready to take off. "Your oil is good and so are your tires. I just put the right amount of air in them. May I ask where you're going Ms. Spivey?" I looked up at him and told him where and why I was going to Minnesota. "I need to get out sometimes. I work hard and I don't have to go back to school until September. I've seen enough fireworks on the Fourth. I just want to do something different you know?" he said and kept on laughing. "What's funny Bryce?" "Nothing, you sound like me. All I do is work. I don't go to school yet, but I attend church, go to work, and go home and workout. I wish I was tagging along with you and your man." *"Is he flirting with me? I didn't say I was going with my man,"* I thought to myself. "Well maybe you don't want me to know, but I know a pretty lady like yourself got somebody and he's a fool if he let you go that far away from home with your home girl," he said and pierced my eyes waiting for my response. I swallowed the large lump that formed in my throat watching his expressions. "I'm a free woman and if I want to go on a vacation with my friend girl than I guess I can do that. Can't I?" "Ex-x-x-cuse me?" he said. We both laughed. His smile could freeze a scorned woman's heart in seconds. His mannerism was pleasant and intriguing. *"Back up hormones..."* I thought to myself. I recognize that he's coming on to me in his subtle way. In seconds, thoughts marched in my head like an army cadet in training. Thoughts like, "is Bryce insecure? He couldn't be? He wasn't arrogant at all. If I were a bit younger or hornier than a pair of thongs waiting to be worn; I would jump on the open opportunity?" I had things to do and somebody else to get rid of. Besides, as handsome as he may be, he probably flirts with any decent looking woman that came in the garage store. "Well, Bryce. It was nice to meet you and thank you for the inspection. How much do I owe you for your services?" He put his hand up to his head pretending as if he were concentrating hard. "Let's see. How about a date with me?" "A date?" "Yes ma'am." My ego hurried up and screamed, yes, but my maturity said hell no. "Don't you have somebody your age to mess with?" I asked pretending not to be flattered. "What do you mean my age? I prefer older women. You're my age?" "Am not," I corrected him. "How old are you if you don't mind me asking?" "None of your business. And I rest my case youngster." I attempted to open my car door to leave the scene with the last word, but he pushed my hand to shut the door. "Do you go to church?" he asked me, I paused. I was surprised that he would ask; I was intrigued that this handsome youngster was a pure gentleman and concerned about my spiritual walk. Could he be the placebo that God would use to cure me from Lovely's controlling substance? Or could he be the one shot antidote to heal the left over pain from all of the rest?

I remembered asking God for a favor not too long ago. I asked for a man who loved Him so that he could love me. Though I didn't attend church on a regular, I adopted the belief that if a man could love and respect God, he could do right by me and I would do right by him. I didn't care if he had an eye on his back or a butt on his face; I desired a God fearing, God loving man. I might not be ready for him spiritually speaking, but from what I've witnessed from the few and far, I would rather have a man of God any day. In the meanwhile, I silently prayed and kept my fingers crossed, hoping whomever he'd be that he wouldn't be too bad on my eyes. If Bryce is the one I know that God hears because he was designed so well, with that rich browned skin, deep big eyes that

Dating My Dad

made me moist whenever I gazed into them. He had a smile that could light up the darkest tunnel. Bryce put the "t" in tall and the "h" in handsome. I speculated him to be around one hundred and ninety-five pounds of playground, just as I craved them.

Nevertheless, I stood blank instead of answering his question. I couldn't separate his approach. I wasn't about to make a fool out of myself assuming him to be interested in me when he was probably a churchy person on a mission to increase his member's points by bringing in new lost souls. Either way, he had gained my attention. I had been asked to go everywhere else but church; I've been asked to go to the movies, the mall, out to dinner, and mostly to go to bed, those offers came on a regular.

Thanks to Lovely and his mess, I've been celibate for a month. I made a vow to stop putting myself in sticky situations, being alone with a man. Any kind of uncomfortable affairs that I have fallen for in the past was enough lessons for my behind. I was tired of coming out of relationships with broken bones, a wet tail, wasted time and a broken heart to show for it. However, going to church sounds pretty safe and neutral. Besides, I hadn't been in a few months of Sundays, I could use a spiritual plunging. "No, I don't go, but I'd like to go with you," I finally answered in a soft accepting tone. "Good, what's your full name again?" "Shelby Spivey and yours?" He wrote my name down on his business card and looked up at me then paused. "Bryce Fitzgerald, please to meet you again Ms. Spivey. What's your address?" "Why don't you call me in a few days when I get back in town and I'll give you my address then? I don't care, cute or not, religious or not, Bryce was human and capable of all of the unknowns and he wasn't going to get my address knowing I was going to be out of town for a while so he could break into my house and lift everything I've worked so hard for. I wish I would! "Okay Ms. Lady, I'll do that. I'll call you when I think you're back in town from your trip. If you don't mind, where are you going? "Chicago," I lied. He should have paid attention. "Okay, well don't forget about me and don't make any decisions or give out your phone number to any more men until you get back to me first. The Lord wants your full-undivided attention. He's got something special waiting for you." "Okay Mr. Fitzgerald, I won't do a thang 'til I get home." I smiled. "Can I get a hug?" he asked as he opened his arms wide and waited. I hugged him though I didn't want to. It was a friendly hug. When we separated, he opened my car door, I got in, he shut my door and I turned the key put it in R and then D and drove off.

My trip could've been ruined had it not been for Desiree flirting with some local men. I thought about Bryce the entire time. The Minnesota mall was nice to see, plus we met some guys from Detroit that told us about the happenings there so we drove on over there and had a ball. The Freak Out picnic in Detroit, it was full of handsome youngsters from all over the country dressed to impress, but my mind was stuck on stupid thoughts about Bryce and me. I kept sounding out our name collaboration as if we were married. I imagined his eyes gazing into mine and his bright smile with his warm hands touching me as he sincerely proposed to me. I took my hope for our tomorrows four hundred miles away with me like I had known him for years. I didn't know what he did to me to cause me to skip out on all of the excitement that was going on, but he had me captivated.

Finally, after a couple rounds of good daiquiris, my fire was lit and I was ready to prowl. Earlier that day, we had to go shopping at the mall because we packed our best outfits and shoes and were still years behind the native Detroit women. They didn't play around when it came to fashion. Before they left out the house they made sure they were well put together. The native men were stylish and riding real nice. We were use to seeing rich Caucasians having what they were driving on a regular.

Desiree and I left our hotel rooms in a mess just to make it to the happy hour at Tuck's down the way from where we stayed. The food was good and fried and the drinks were big and tasty. Truth be told, I was glad we had separate rooms. Desiree was my girl, but she could get a bit loose whenever she had too much to drink. And I didn't feel like babysitting her or entertaining any strangers for her while she'd be throwing up or stretched out across the bed drunk. It was our last night in Detroit and I wanted to mingle. I wanted to network and connect with some interesting people, maybe some lifetime friends from someplace else that I could say I know and traveled across states to visit. "Shelby, I don't want to go home tomorrow. I met this dude from Atlanta, Georgia and he's got a suite for the next few days. He says we can stay with him if we need to, free of charge." She gave, coming from I don't know where 20 minutes ago. I caught myself rolling my eyes at her. "Who is this prince charming Dezie?" "He went to the back to order us some food and he'll be over here to buy us drinks. Tell me what you think, okay." "What I think about what?" "What you think about him?" she asked as she burst out laughing. I smiled too. "What's happening ladies?" a familiar voice greeted from behind us. When I turned around and saw it was Lovely, my eyes bucked and my heart thumped. I didn't expect to see him there. He hadn't mentioned that he would be going to the Freak Out festival. "Hey what's up with you sir?" I nonchalantly greeted. "How long have you been up here?" I jumped in before he started. My pulse pumped, causing me to get pissed off wondering if he had been in Detroit from the first day of the event and didn't inform me. "Gimme kisses Shelby Baby?" I leaned in poking my lips out for a peck quickly to get right back to my question. "How long you been here, Mr. Lovely?" I cleared my throat and waited. Desiree hopped up on the bar stool next to me and crossed her legs. "Slow you row Shelby Baby. You know I don't like all those questions. You happy to see me? Since Tuesday, Shelby Baby. My partners and I had some business to take care of up here. What you drinking?" he switched. I ordered a top shelf Long Island Ice Tea and asked Desiree what she wanted. For a brief couple of minutes, I forgot about Bryce, but it wasn't long before I was thinking about him again. My body was near Lovely; way up in Detroit in Tuck's, laughing and having a good time, but my heart took its own road trip back home to the parking lot with Bryce. I sensed that Lovely was no match for Bryce. He had come on to the field and hit a home run while Lovely had been on the team, but lost his starting position.

    I know Lovely thought it to be strange that I turned down his offer to spend the night with him in his suite. I wasn't feeling him, for one thing, I was feeling Bryce. Two, I didn't like the new distance between us and all the mysterious things that have been going on. And three, him gawking at Desiree didn't make things any easier. Hard for me to believe, but I didn't care. Lovely was full of it and I was tired of smelling it. Plus, whenever he didn't get his way, he was capable of making things messy and miserable for the person who didn't say yes to his request. Knowing him the way I do, he was probably staring at her to make me jealous. There were too many beautiful women around for him to go for my friend.

I made it through the rest of the festival with a smile on my face. Desiree made sure I had just as much fun as she did. Lovely disappeared after his disappointment with me. We met some really interesting people from other states that had the potential to become great road trips with happy endings. All though I got a kick out of Minneapolis, I had the most fun in Detroit; I couldn't relocate and settle in Detroit like Desiree claimed she planned to do within the next five years. If she goes through with it I'll visit her for a spell, but I would not ever leave Milwaukee, Wisconsin.

I dropped my bags to the kitchen floor and ran to my bedroom to grab the phone. My fingers were burning to dial Bryce's number. The phone rang and rang then finally a voice answers, "Parts, can I help you?" I exhaled, "May I speak to Bryce please?" "I'm sorry he's not here today, he's off." "*Damn.*" "When do you expect him back, please?" "Ma'am I can't give out that information. Is there something I can help you with?" "Oh, umm, no thank you. Could you tell him that Shelby called please?" "I sure will. He has your number?" "Yes, he has my number. Thank you." "Okay then have a nice day ma'am." I hung up. I sobbed a bit, falling back onto my bed. I wanted to speak with him so badly. I don't know when I'll talk to him again. I wish I had his home phone number. He gave me his work number because he said he's always at work, but the first time I tried to call him, he wasn't there. I peeled myself from the bed and went to the refrigerator for a drink. Just as I thought, Regina cleaned me out. That's why I'm glad I bought stuff for her and told her it was mine. I nabbed my purse and keys and headed out the house for the store. Although the grocery store was about a mile from my home, I took a three-mile detour pass Bryce's job. I just wanted to see if he might have shown up. I didn't have the courage to go in so I drove off and went to the grocery store across the way. There was a good reason I didn't shop at this store; they were overpriced. What you can get 2 for $1 in the hood was almost three dollars there. I walked around trying to make myself buy something, but every time I checked the price, I changed my mind. I ended up buying a two-liter Pepsi for $2.00. I wasn't about to get caught coming out of the store empty handed, just in case somebody from the auto parts store saw me. I glared over in the direction of his store to see if I could spot him then jumped in my ride before the rain poured down.

"When you get back stranger?" Regina asked me as I shook myself free of the rain. "A little while ago. I went to the store to get something to drink, there was nothing left. Did you miss me Momma?" I asked while taking my clothes off at the door in front of my mother like I did as a child. "I guess you can say that Shelby. I had an awesome time at the church over the weekend. Deacon Brown blew the roof off with his awesome preaching. Who knew he had it in em?" "Oh yeah. Momma you like that church don't you. I'm so proud of you finding something you enjoy and sticking to it. I missed you Momma." "When you're doing the Lord's service, you don't think of it as work, it's just a way of life Shelby. I miss you too." "Momma did anyone call me?" I asked as I walked pass her half-naked. "You know I don't answer that phone when you ain't here. What I'ma answer your phone for and I got my own calls to answer?" "Momma, did anyone call me?" I turned to her giving her a serious look

Dating My Dad

knowing good and well she answers my phone. "Some boy called a few times, but I don't remember his name." "How do you know it was the same one?" "Cause I looked at the Caller ID and he called from the same number trying to disguise his voice." I ran to the phone to check the Caller ID. Someone did call eight times from the same number, but I didn't recognize the phone number at all. There was a few other familiar numbers, but the only message left was a marketer. "Yeah Momma, I'ma go with you next week. I'm about to get in the bed after I take a bath. I love you and I'll talk to you in the morning," I hollered back as she was leaving out the door. I got up from the couch and ran to get a drink and went back to call the strange number to see whom it was. "Hello, did someone call for Shelby from this number?" I paused and waited for the lady to answer. "I don't know any Shelby honey. Maybe one of my chillrens called ya playing on the phone." "What are your children's name ma'am, if you don't mind me asking?" she said as she took a deep breath. "I do mind!" And she hung up in my face. That Witch! I was just trying to see who called me from that number. I know Lovely's woman isn't that old and he wasn't that bold to call me from his house. Maybe it was some kids playing on the phone? If it were one of my friend girls they would've left a long drawn out message eight times. Oh well, I jumped in the hot bathtub full of Epson Salt letting the honey melt off my skin as I sunk down. I thought about what Bryce would be doing, then thought about Lovely, then right back to Bryce. If only he knew how much he was on my mind, he would call me.

To be continued…

ABOUT THE AUTHOR

Apple Dailey was born and raised in Milwaukee, Wisconsin, but later in her life decided to trust the Voice within and leave everything and everybody she knew, heading to a place she knew nothing of; Texas where she resides. She was so pleased that she listened to the voice inside her; it was Texas where her new life began. She picked up her pen and pad again.

Currently, she does presentations bringing awareness of domestic violence. Apple is on a mission to end this growing epidemic; speaking for those who cannot speak for themselves. She is also working on her second novel; part two of the Trauma Bond Series.

She would love to come where you are and share her story to help. For bookings, please feel free to contact Apple at appledailey.com.